D1459147

NORTHAMPTONSHIRE
CENTRAL LIBRARY

− 8 JAN 2007

TA

− 1 FEB 2007

25/5/13

2 8 MAR 2007
1 8 MAY 2007
1 3 JUN 2007
1 2 OCT 2007

1 7 DEC 2007

1 2 MAY 2009

80 002 645 274

TARTING
RIATHLON

Mike Barfield

THE CROWOOD PRESS

First published in 2006 by
The Crowood Press Ltd
Ramsbury, Marlborough
Wiltshire SN8 2HR

www.crowood.com

© Mark Barfield 2006

All rights reserved. No part of this publication may be reproduced or
transmitted in any form or by any means, electronic or mechanical,
including photocopy, recording, or any information storage and
retrieval system, without permission in writing from the publishers.

British Library Cataloguing-in-Publication Data
A catalogue record for this book is available from the
British Library.

ISBN   1 86126 875 0
EAN   978 1 86126 875 4

Acknowledgements
The author would like to thank Nigel Farrow for photography, Paul
Moss for technical support, Norman Brook for inspiration and
Nicola Barfield for emotional support.

Disclaimer
Please note that the author and the publisher of this book do not
accept any responsibility whatsoever for any error or omission, nor
any loss, injury, damage, adverse outcome or liability suffered as a
result of the information contained in this book, or reliance upon it.
Since the Triathlon can be dangerous and could involve physical
activities that are too strenuous for some individuals to engage in
safely, it is essential that a doctor be consulted before undertaking
training.

NORTHAMPTONSHIRE LIBRARIES	
802645274	
Bertrams	28.10.06
796.4257	£12.99
854511	NC

Typeset by Florence Production Ltd, Stoodleigh, Devon

Printed and bound in Singapore by Craft Print International Ltd

ontents

Foreword

Triathlon is a fantastic sport and one that is inspiring and challenging for all. I would like to encourage as many people as possible to take up the challenge of triathlon and feel that reading *Starting Triathlon* and working through the process outlined within the book will help people reach a starting point to achieve their goals.

Triathlon is a very rewarding sport that can change people's lives for the better.

I hope that this book makes the sport 1 accessible for more athletes and also th many novices as possible are able to racing after reading it. Hopefully they find triathlon as exciting and rewardir I have.

Jodie Swa
Elite Triat
Olympic Games 2

ntroduction

thlon has been around for more than
ity years. The original concept is sur-
ided in myth and mystery, although most
e that it came from three friends dis-
ing which sport is the hardest: swim-
g, cycling or running. To resolve the
ment it was agreed that a race com-
ng all three disciplines should be under-
n. Legend has it this was based on the
aii Open Water swim race, the Hawaii
race and the Hawaii Marathon – and
e Hawaii Ironman triathlon was born.
e years that have passed since this infa-
s inception, the sport of triathlon has
ved and changed. The long-distance
ts are now only a small part of the huge
ty of events open to potential triathletes.
thlon has developed enormously and is
a high-profile sport that has been part
e Olympic Games since Sydney in 2000.
also a mass-participation activity with
ts taking place in the UK that accom-
ate more than 6,000 athletes. Given the
ty of formats and distances, anyone who
undertaken even modest preparatory
ing can take part. There are races of
length from the relatively short sprint
nces to the long-distance Ironman
ts, ensuring that triathlon can appeal to
y wide range of athletes. Triathlon can
accommodate competitors of all stand-
your target may be to complete your
sprint event and simply to enjoy the
t, or you may be racing against yourself
challenge. At the other extreme, you
be an aspiring elite athlete looking to
pete against the best in the country or
world. Or you may come in between,
g sport very seriously and making a com-
nent to become the best triathlete in

your age group. This is certainly possible as
triathlon enables you to compete in age
groups against your peers on a national,
European and even a world stage.

Just one event gives all these possibilities.
Triathlon has seen a huge increase in both
the number of people participating in events,
and the number and diversity of the events
themselves. It draws athletes from all areas.
Swimmers, runners and cyclists find it
appealing for a huge variety of reasons, while
single-discipline athletes find the added
attraction of training across three disciplines
prevents boredom by adding variety to a
training programme that may have become
a little monotonous. Many participants
enter the sport for health reasons. Gyms and
health clubs promote participation in triathlon as part of a healthy lifestyle, seeing
triathlon as ideal for motivating their cus-
tomers to lose weight and get in shape. Many
successful athletes started in this way and
then went on to become the best in their
age groups.

The aim of this book is to help you identify and achieve your triathlon goals by taking
a systematic approach to planning, analysing
each discipline and the demands it places on
the individual, and then ascertaining what
skills need to be mastered in order to progress
within each of the individual sports. If you
are a swimmer who is bored of the routine
and wants a new challenge, a runner who
needs to add variety to training to prevent
injury, or a cyclist in need of a new way of
competing, this book will help you capitalize
on your strengths and work on your weaknesses. Or if you are a complete beginner
with little, or no, experience of physical
activity or sport, we will take you through

planning of your training and competi-
programme, examine in great detail the
ng you will need to undertake, help you
re that you avoid injury, and then guide
progress to the start line and on to a
ssful race finish.

tention will be paid to the detailed con-
tion of a realistic training programme
fits in with your lifestyle and helps you
ve your aspirations. It will help you
e goals and set realistic, yet challenging,
ts to motivate you, whether you just
to complete the event or have a spe-
determination to beat a certain time in
selected event. Each discipline will be
en down into detailed components and
ill examine the equipment you will need.
close look at the specific skills necessary
in each discipline will ensure that you
ot waste time and effort and that you
smartly. The development of your phys-
bilities or fitness and conditioning will
be looked at in some detail in order to
you understand what is required. By
essing your weaknesses and guiding you
ugh the myths of training using the
ication of sports science and sound
hing principles, your progression to race
will be made as efficient as possible. We
help you to understand how to move
een the disciplines on race day in the
useful and effective way. There will be
guidance on nutrition and the lifestyle
ace that will help to ensure that triathlon
mes a part of your life, but not neces-
the guiding force in your life.

LAINING TRIATHLON

chlon is a multi-sport event comprising
ming, cycling and running. The athlete
s with the swim and covers the course
istance in either a pool or open water,
as lake or the sea. The athlete then
s the water and moves directly to the
section of the race, before progressing
ght into the run. Each transfer between

Exiting an open water swim, one of the most
exciting aspects of triathlon racing.

disciplines takes place in a transition area and
is part of the race. The total time taken to
cover the distances from the start of the swim
to the completion of the run section is the
finishing time for the race. There are a
number of variations to this theme, including
duathlon (run, bike, run) and aquathlon
(swim-run), and races may cover a wide range
of distances. There are also off-road and
cross-country events, and even gym-based
static triathlons, usually used as taster events
or run during the closed season to help satisfy
the craving for triathlon.

The great majority of triathlon events are
non-drafting, which means that during the
cycle section of the race riders must not

ng page: Age-group athletes in a competitive situation during a race's final phase.

directly follow each other and there must be a gap of 5m between athletes' bikes. This ensures that riders do not benefit from the energy saved by riding directly behind another cyclist and therefore the event is fair for all athletes.

Elite races, however, generally allow drafting, as do a number of events in which non-elite athletes may compete. Non-elite athletes are classified as those competing in an age group category. The category entitled elite is often used but rarely understood. In the context of this book it refers to those athletes who are recognized by British Triathlon (the governing body of triathlon in the UK) as being among the best in the country. Within the age group categories athletes will, in fact, generally end up racing against athletes of all age groups, but the results are presented in a format that displays both an athlete's position overall and where they came in comparison to their peers. simply means that results are compared only with the overall results for the e but also within an individual's own age sex) group. Age groups are classified in year increments from twenty upwards. allows much more realistic comparisons provides any individual with the opportu to progress within their own age categ There are national championships for ath competing within their age groups number of distances, as well as duath There are also European and world triat championships that accommodate age g athletes and present world champion medals: these races are normally run on day before the elite event but in the s venue and on the same course, somet that is unique to triathlon. Many races have novice categories allowing inex enced athletes the opportunity to com

Triathlons can be held in some of the world's most attractive locations.

other first-time triathletes; many of
e even offer prizes to novices. If you
aspirations to compete as either an elite
lete or as an age group athlete repre-
ng your country at European or inter-
nal championships, the webpage of
national governing body (www.british
hlon.org) contains all the information
will need.

here are a number of ways for prospec-
riathletes to find a suitable event to take
in. National magazines generally carry
sive lists of multi-sport events and can
ide a great deal of information con-
ing the type of event you are looking at
the facilities provided around the event.
ebsites of national governing bodies,
as British Triathlon, also carry details
e events that they sanction, providing
y of information to help you decide if
event is right for you. British Triathlon
publishes an annual handbook that
ains detailed information on all the
ts registered with them and lists the
act details for entries. Triathlon clubs
also be able to advise you about local
ts and can provide help and advice with
pment and additional training sessions.
e than three hundred triathlon clubs
lished in the UK are listed both on the
sh Triathlon website and in its hand-
k. Triathlon clubs can provide a great
of support to the novice triathlete and
be able to offer advice on equipment
race entry that will supplement that pro-
d within this book. Many triathlon clubs
run training sessions that can be used
ugment the programme we will be for-
ating later on. However, care must be
n when accessing additional coaching
ce. It is essential to ensure that any
h you start working with is both aware
our goals and background and under-
ds the process you are working through.
ches must also be appropriately quali-
The most suitable qualification for a
h working with a triathlete in the UK is
British Triathlon Association's coaching
d, which is issued at levels from one
ugh to five. If you are receiving basic
s-based structured training sessions

Whatever age group you belong to, there is the
possibility of representing your country.

within a club the minimum standard you
should be looking for is level two. A level
one coach may work with you only under
the supervision of a level two coach or
another at an even higher level. If you are
looking for a coach to help you design your
training programme, a level three coach
should be the minimum standard acceptable.
Coaches from the single disciplines will also
be able to help you especially with the skills
required in the individual sports. Again
you must make your coaches aware of your
background, goals and other training commitments, and you must ensure that they are

appropriately qualified as triathlon coaches to the levels described above. With all of this in place you will find triathlon clubs can be a tremendous source of support, encouragement and knowledge, making the process you are about to start much more fun.

Triathlons take place over a wide variety of distances:

	Swim	Cycle	Run
Sprint	750m	20km	5km
Standard	1,500m	40km	10km
Middle	2,500m	80km	20km
Long	4,000m	130km	30km

There are also many events that do not fit into these classes, and plenty of smaller, pool-based, novice events are held over shorter distances than these.

Before choosing your first event should consider your previous athletic ex ence, the time you have available to and period remaining between now and chosen event. Less experienced athletes be best advised to participate in a sh event, although with sufficient time, and right volume of training, standard dist events are well within reach. Middle and distance events may not be ideal as f time triathlons, although there are plenty of athletes who have taken the step into triathlon with these kinds of eve Your individual strengths within the t disciplines may play a large part in your sion to choose a particular event, but al all your chosen event must be excitin you and motivate you sufficiently to pu the training hours that will be requi Aquathlons and duathlons are also well w

While exciting, the concept of open water can be daunting. Duathlon may ease you into the multi-sport environment.

e spectacle in sport, but not for the faint-hearted.

idering, either as target events in their right or as stepping-stones to a full tri-n. These events, particularly duathlons, often held towards the beginning and of the racing season, which generally ches from April through to September, can be a great way of testing your com-petition skills and refining your preparation for events. There are also many midweek duathlons that can be used both to develop skills and add some excitement to a training programme.

CHAPTER 1
Planning

The old adage 'fail to prepare, prepare to fail' is truly accurate for an endurance sporting event such as triathlon. Whether you have a successful race day or a disappointing, and possibly painful, experience is often determined many months prior to the event. A sensible and realistic approach with a hint of ambition, combined with a fair bit of dedication and determination, will get you to race day in the right physical and mental state to ensure you have the best possible chance of succeeding. However, before you can succeed in your goals you must first set some.

In the introduction I briefly outlined the different types of events and will now provide a little more detail in order to help you choose an event.

AQUATHLON

These events sometimes consist of a run followed by a swim followed by a run but you will also see 'run followed by swim' aquathlons. There are set distances for aquathlon events, but because these events are often used for novices these distances are rarely followed. The standard distance for aquathlon is a 2.5km run, a 1km swim and a 2.5km run. Long distance is 5km run, 2km swim, 5km run. Aquathlons are run in both swimming pools and in open water (lakes, rivers or sea). They often take place in early or late season or as part of novice or children's taster events. This is mainly because they are easier to take part in, as participants require no bikes. There are national and world championships in aquathlon, but the profile of aquathlon is not as high as that of

triathlon or duathlon. These are good ev to help build up to the full triathlon and be really useful in developing swimming transition skills.

DUATHLON

This comprises a run followed by a bike and a second, generally shorter, run. Natic

Planning covers many angles and preparation the key to success in triathlon.

...lon has the highest profile of all the multi-sport formats.
...like this explain why.

...pean and World championships are held
...uathletes and the event has a good
...e. Many athletes specialize in duathlon
...here is a national series of events in the
...There are set distances for duathlon:
...ard distance is 10km run, 40km cycle,
...run, and long distance is (not less than)
...run, 60km cycle, 10km run.
...any clubs also run events during
...ner evenings, so giving athletes the
...rtunity to compete and get high-quality
...ng at the same time. Because there is
...eed to hire a swimming pool it is obvi-
...a little easier to organize duathlon
...s. The nature of duathlon favours a
...g runner and athletes from a distance
...ng background will probably find
...lon an easier option, though the experi-
...of running after completing a hard sec-
...of cycling must be experienced and
...d not be underestimated. If you choose
...lon as your target event the structure

of your training may well be very different,
although most of the principles detailed else-
where in this book will be applicable.

TRIATHLON

This is the main focus of this book and the
multi-sport option with the highest profile.
I have briefly mentioned the race distances
in the introduction but it will be helpful to
look more closely at the types of event that
are available.

The major triathlon races and all national,
European and international championships
take place in open water. This is any piece
of water, such as the sea or a lake, river,
dock or reservoir, that is big enough (and
safe enough) for the swimmer to complete
the required distance. The concept of swimming in this kind of water for swimmers who
have been raised and trained in swimming

pools can be both daunting and exciting. This can be enough to put many people off taking part in triathlon, even though open water swimming, while it is a very different experience from swimming in a controlled environment such as a pool, is a remarkable experience. However, if you are dead set against open water swimming there are plenty of pool events, especially in the earlier and later part of the racing season, although these events will generally be shorter in distance than those held in open water. There are some notable differences between pool versus open water swimming. In pool events you will generally be swimming in a laned pool. You will start in a lane and, while there may be other people in the lane, there will be little need for physical contact with other swimmers as events are generally sufficiently well organized to allow swimmers the best opportunity to cover the set distance unhindered by the other competitors. Open water swims generally involve a mass start, which means you will be setting off with a group of other swimmers. In small events this may be all of the competitors at once, but in larger events it will be a group organized by age group, experience or by race number. Starting a swim with a large group is a specific skill that we will discuss in the swim skills section, but swimming in this way is unique to triathlon.

In the UK, open water swimming will require a wetsuit. The race rules stipulate that with a water temperature of above 14°C wetsuits are optional. There are also combinations of race distances and water temperatures above 22°C when wetsuits are not allowed. Unless you target a race abroad you are likely to need to a wetsuit: help in selecting a wetsuit if you choose to enter an open water event will be found in Chapter 2. Swimming in a wetsuit will require some practice and will be covered below, together with the other specific skills of swimming for triathlon. Pool-based triathlons are generally shorter events, few being longer than sprint distance. As wetsuits are not allowed for pool-based events, this is one less piece of equipment you will need, making pool-based events more accessible. This also makes them

a good option for a first experience o athlon over shorter distances and the generally run in easily accessible le centres with good facilities for both petitors and spectators.

TESTING YOURSELF

As we have already seen, there is a hug ference between the shortest and the lo set distances. In fact there are many ev especially pool-based triathlons, that shorter swims than those stated. Ther you have a choice of events, from some that could last around an hour to one can take up most of the day. This can it difficult to choose an event, althou sensible approach will help. A very long plan covering a number of years will br novice from sedentary status to Iroi athlete with plenty of small goals in betv

Open water swims present interesting challe not least the exit from the water.

then the time is probably less important, though the time is still worth recording. When conducting these tests ensure that you are fresh, have had sufficient to eat and drink (*see* Chapter 7) and that you are not going to be impeded by poor equipment. Undertake each test on a different day as you will not yet be ready to start combining events, and at this stage that ability is not yet relevant.

In each discipline set off at a steady pace rather than what you would perceive as race pace. The objective at this stage is to test your endurance rather than your speed. If you are a competent athlete in any of the three disciplines then record your PB times next to some relevant distances, for example times for 400m, 750m, 1,500m and up to 3.5km for the swim, 10km, 20km, 40km on the bike and 5km, 10km, 20km and 40km for the run. This will provide a reasonable assessment of your strength and give you a clear idea of your starting point and priorities for training.

Establishing your starting points		
	Distance covered without stopping	*Time taken*
Swim		
Bike		
Run		

...nlon is for everybody and sensible targeting ...elp you complete your race.

...r aspirations can be allowed to dictate ... goals, but a realistic approach to what ...can achieve is also required.

...n order to work out some reasonable ...s you need to establish your starting ...t. You must have a realistic idea of what ...can currently do. This means distances ...er than times.

...) if you have some experience of run-..., what distances can you cover? Similarly ... swimming and cycling, what experience ...ou have and what distances can you ...r? In order to answer these questions ... may need to do some tests in each ...pline. If completion is your aspiration

REALISTIC PLANNING

With this exercise complete you can start on your planning. By now you may have an idea of the kind of event you want to focus on. It is at this point that a little mathematics needs to be added to your training to establish a realistic programme and timescale.

Although there are many different ways of scheduling training, one aspect that coaches always agree upon is that there must be sufficient rest. It is essential to incorporate rest and easy periods into your training,

Working out where and when to train in advance will make this challenge achievable.

allowing at least one very easy or complete rest day every week. (For how to schedule your training into your week, *see* Chapter 7.) Many programmes also work in an easy week on a regular basis – generally one easy week every four to six weeks. It is not always practical to stick rigidly to one easy week in four, as this may not fit in with your work, family and social life, so a more flexible approach is required. This is important at this stage because a number of examples will be examined in order to demonstrate the planning process with this week-by-week structure in

mind. The objective will be to work tow a weekly progressing guide of 10 per c This means that weekly training vol and/or distance should not be increase more than 10 per cent per week. As progress the duration for given volume start to drop, but, even with this in m planning to increase distance by no r than 10 per cent a week and fitting in easy weeks around work, family and s life should mean that injuries ought t avoided as far as possible. There should be time left over to tackle issues as they or to take the distance achieved in trai to 120 per cent of race distance, giving confidence to the athlete.

Example 1

An athlete can swim 100m without stopp run for 10 minutes (approx. just under 2 and cycle for about 10km. The target eve a sprint distance race (750m, 20km, 5kn

- To bring the swim endurance up to required distance at an increase of 10 cent per week will take 22 weeks
- To bring the cycling endurance up to required distance at an increase of 10 cent per week will take 8 weeks
- To bring the running endurance up to required distance at an increase of 10 cent per week will take 10 weeks

It may be possible to progress faster this but the risk of injury is increased. I been established that swimming is relat the weakest discipline and therefore req more time to develop. When the di: lines are examined more closely within planning section, more detailed infor tion will be provided about how n sessions should be targeted in a week how these should be filled. Working in easy weeks, our programme should between twenty-six and twenty-eight w

Facing page: Triathlon is an endurance event to reach your goal you must put in the volur of training.

including the easy week prior to the event itself. With this in mind, you can work out which events you can enter based on the time you will need to complete the required distance.

Example 2

An athlete can swim 500m without stopping, is a competent runner with a PB for 10km of 46 minutes and can cycle for about 15km. The target event is a standard distance race (1,500m, 40km, 10km).

The volume invested in cycling will be repai on race day.

Triathlon can be a great spectator sport for family and friends, who need to be involved as you plan and work towards your goal.

- To bring the swim endurance up to required distance at an increase of 1 cent per week will take 12 weeks
- To bring the cycling endurance up t required distance at an increase of 1 cent per week will take 12 weeks
- The running is at a standard sufficie the event and therefore this will be i tained by the training programme r than developed

The events outside the running are ec balanced and, working in the easy weeks programme should take between fou and fifteen weeks.

nple 3

thlete can swim 50m without stopping,
·un for only about 3 minutes (0.5km)
can cycle for 30 minutes (8km). This
te is new to physical activity and has
ted a middle-distance target event
)0m, 80km, 20km).

› bring the swim endurance up to the
quired distance at an increase of 10 per
nt per week will take 42 weeks
› bring the cycling endurance up to the
quired distance at an increase of 10 per
nt per week will take 25 weeks
› bring the running endurance up to the
quired distance at an increase of 10 per
nt per week will take 40 weeks

events are similarly balanced. Although
ycling should come a little easier, it does
more time out on the road covering the
nce to build up to the required levels.
king in the easy weeks, our programme
ld take between forty-nine and fifty-
weeks.

›me of these periods are very long and
should consider the time demanded by
y, work and social commitments such
·lidays. The total required by these activ-
should be added to the overall time
lule. This method may seem very cau-
but it will result in delivering an athlete
event without incurring injury and in
idition that will ensure that he or she
·njoy the day and complete the race. If
are targeting a particular event, then,
ding it fits inside the minimum time to
·ve the race distance that you have cal-
·ed, based on the test and formula we
suggested, you will be able to work
·ds that specific event. If you have more
this allows a little bit of breathing space
·commodate factors external to your
·ing, such as work, family and minor
·s. Less time than you calculate for this
·ng period can place you under pressure
may result in a situation where you
·)ach the event without sufficient prepar-
·, so increasing the risk of injury or not
·)leting the event.

If you have no option but to cut the time,
progress as indicated over the weeks by
increasing distances as suggested and, later
in the programme, allow greater increases in
distance and volume, and perhaps also intensity. Early on the body may not be ready to
accommodate the load placed upon it and it
may therefore break down into either injury
or illness. If this happens it will have a much
more debilitating effect on a shorter programme than it could have on a longer
training programme.

FITTING IT IN

At this stage, and while working through the
next section, we will be developing the
outline of your training plan in terms of how
many weeks you will need for training. To
refine this plan further we need to look
closely at when you will be training during
an average week. If you have a very set
routine, and can predict from week to week
when you are working and where you will
be, this exercise will be fairly similar. If you
have a varied working pattern, are often
changing work plans or are working shifts,
however, it may be more appropriate to
repeat this exercise regularly to ensure you
can fit in your training.

The accompanying chart will help you
identify when you can train. Fill it in by
writing against the hours when you are busy.
Try to include everything: work, travel, rest,
eating, socializing, family time, study, and
anything else that occupies your time. Be
very, very honest – if this exercise is to be
successful you must complete the form accu-
rately. Once you have completed this task
you may find that training opportunities
present themselves. If this is the case, that's
great. If not, and you find there are no reasonable gaps in your day, then you may need
to start rearranging your week.

Many people train before the start of the
working day. If you are able to do this there
are many advantages, since your training is
out of the way and will not get moved or
cancelled as the day's events unfold. This
time is often quieter at facilities – whether

Planning your training week

	Mon	Tue	Wed	Thur	Fri	Sat	Sun
0500							
0530							
0600							
0630							
0700							
0730							
0800							
0830							
0900							
0930							
1000							
1030							
1100							
1130							
1200							
1230							
1300							
1330							
1400							
1430							
1500							
1530							
1600							
1630							
1700							
1730							
1800							
1830							
1900							
1930							
2000							
2030							
2100							
2130							
2200							

it, and the quality of sleep experienced after training in the evening versus watching TV for three hours has to be experienced.

Shift workers and those whose week changes regularly through the demands of family, study or work will need a different approach to exercise. Training and accommodating shift work and all the other commitments in life requires an extra measure of discipline. Many shift workers follow a regular pattern over a number of weeks and so it may be possible to do a number of the charts to find out when you can train during a given shift period. Night shifts can play havoc with the body clock and a week when an athlete is on nights may not be the best for an intense training block. Indeed it may be more suitable to choose this as

ultimate goal during long training hours.

, pool or track – and you should feel after a good night's sleep. Training in morning does not suit everyone and it often be a good idea to experiment and the time of day when you feel best able ain. Lunch-time training is also popular many people. If your day can accommodate this it can be a great time to fit in a or a swim. Again this may not suit you, it should be considered when seeking the opportunities you have to train n your week.

or many people the evening is the key to train. This is when sports clubs meet raining and the bulk of athletes will end oing at least some of their training in vening. This may mean sacrificing tele- n time but the rewards will be well worth

Tim Don in full flight.

your rest/easy week. Careful attention to nutrition during shift work will improve the ability to accommodate the training, although it is always more challenging to work a programme around an ever-changing shift pattern. Those with a less regular structure to their lives may be best served by repeating the exercise of planning the weekly training once a week or fortnight. In this way meetings, trips and other factors can be accommodated and training sessions can be planned to fit around the other commitments.

HOW OFTEN AND WHEN?

The question of how often to train is always difficult as it will depend on the individual. As a basic rule shorter, more frequent,

Racing shoulder to shoulder with others will inspire your best performance.

Completing your training volume may not always feel good, but the end result will.

training sessions will pay dividends novices, especially at the beginning of training programme. If your plan is to c the longer events, you will inevitably to conduct a number of long sessions at s point in your training. These are often accommodated at weekends or on full off when the right kind of recovery can place.

At this stage it is best to identify training opportunities in your week and build from there. As an absolute minim one session a week in each discipline enable you to complete an event, g sufficient time to progress and dev endurance. Many athletes train every or on six days out of seven, although novice this will be excessive. As you prog

ing with others
elp maintain your
ation.

r athletes will
exactly how it

you may feel that adding an extra session will enable you to move ahead and this should be incorporated within your week. If you have identified that you have six sessions a week available for exercise, but have no experience of training in the recent past, start with three sessions and build up to six sessions across the disciplines over the next two to three months.

When structuring training into your week you will need to consider exactly when you plan to train in each discipline. Starting from one session in each discipline per week, you will be attempting to work on your weaknesses and build on your strengths. Although it might not worry a complete novice in the early stages of training, as you progress you will start to develop particular strengths, especially if you have some experience within cycling, swimming or running. It can then be tempting to train more in this area, since you may well enjoy it more than the others. This temptation should be avoided.

Strong swimmers who can cover the distance required, but are at only a reasonable level in cycling and feel weak at running, should build on their weekly programme of one session per week in each discipline by developing their weaker disciplines first. This means that the first additional

Pushing yourself to the limit does not always feel good.

GAINING CONFIDENCE

So far I have only really looked at a targ
completing an event. The approach is si
if you have aspirations to achieve a sp
time for a given event, but you must
further considerations into account.

First, you must be competent and
confident about completing the dist
you will be racing over. This process ca
addressed as detailed above. By follo
this training programme you will not
increase your endurance, and so be ab
complete the distance, but you will als
an increase in your speed. This will have
brought about by your improved effici

Racing can become addictive: many athletes
keep on going.

session should be a running session and the
second should be a bike session. If a further session is then added this should probably also be running, and so on. Using this
principle of building sessions into your week,
you can now repeat the exercise above with
some idea of when you will be training in
each discipline, so utilizing the opportunities you have identified within the week's
allocated training slots. You can further allo-
cate these slots to particular disciplines and
perhaps decide on the necessary locations.
At this point you can start to make use of
some of the sessions your local clubs may be
running, as we discussed above. With all of
this now complete you should have a basic
overview of the minimum number of weeks
you need to prepare for a race, what these
weeks will consist of at the start in terms of
training sessions, and how they will develop
as you progress towards your event.

possibly a reduction in body weight,
rs that have a pronounced effect on
ing and cycling.

, you can now complete the distance in
ing and want to get faster. You now
to complete a number of time trials
s the three disciplines. Split the race dis-
into three and complete a time trial in
hree disciplines recording the time at
third, two-thirds and full race distance.
approach to the time trials should be
ar to that of the original test, but this
you are looking to achieve your best
This may take a little practice: initially
may find that you go out too steadily,
ave a lot left in reserve towards the end
e test, or you start very hard and struggle
stain the effort. This is where the meas-
during the test are useful to enable you
e how efficiently you are pacing your-
You will get more useful results if you
certain you are well rested and have
ufficient nutrition and hydration before
ests, especially for longer efforts.

you are targeting longer races, such as
le-distance or long-distance Ironman
ts, it may not be practical to conduct
ime trials across the disciplines. If this is
ase, the race distance that you have
dy divided into three can be covered at
distance and then divided into thirds
this point. This will give an indication
ur performance, but a lot will still rest
the ability to measure your effort
ghout the test, especially bearing in
that nutrition and hydration become
more important over the longer dis-
s.

nce you have conducted the time trials
believe the times reflect your ability
rately and aren't affected adversely by
ability to measure your effort evenly
ghout the event, you have your starting
t. By this stage it will have become
rent in which event(s) you are stronger.
may relate to your past experience as
hlete, but during the initial endurance
ing phase you may have developed
gths in disciplines that previously were
miliar to you. The times from your trials
give you this information.

Targeting a time in a race will require a slick
transition, which takes practice.

INCREASING THE PACE

Data from your trials may also reveal if you
have an issue with pacing, which may be
something that you need to target over the
next phase of your training. The sections of
this book devoted to individual disciplines
will tackle the specific sessions designed to
help you develop additional pace. Although
as a general principle the training will be
of a higher intensity, it may be of a lower
volume. It is probably worth maintaining the
frequency so that the effect on your planned
training time will be negligible and perhaps
the number of training sessions and volume
of training in a given week will not rise. As
before, we need to establish some realistic
targets. This is not as easy as was the case
with the distances, although we still need to
follow the principles of good targeting.

Improvements in race performance will take a focused attitude to training.

The right clothing for the conditions will help with performance in racing and training.

An athlete who has used rest wisely will deliver on race day.

target time should be:

fic to each discipline and to the overall time including transition.

surable either by the measurement of splits taken at specific points during the or by time trials conducted in training.

evable This is the tricky one and, while get should be challenging, it is impos- here to set predicted times that could part of a target based on time trial ts. There are a number of tests that claim able to do this, but none has been rig- sly tested on novice or beginners in tri- on and therefore the accuracy is tionable.

ed This relates to both the performance in the three disciplines and the period in which the goal time is to be achieved.

n the approach has to be very similar hat established for your endurance e. We need to set smaller interim targets monitor progress in this way. Monthly ts are probably most appropriate, with trials scheduled to test your progress. ould be noted that if your time goal is specific event it may not be possible to the actual course. Try to use time trial es and courses that reflect the event and of terrain over which you will be racing. or example, if you are racing an open r triathlon with the cycling section g place on a hilly circuit and the run oad and cross-country, it may not be ful to do the time trials in a pool and on a flat road course for cycling and on ck or hard surfaced area for the run. e realistic data may be obtained by repli- g as closely as possible the race terrain, ving you a clearer idea of race perform- . Weather will also have an effect: when sing data take this into account if a per- ance is significantly better or worse than cted. Did you have to deal with a head or tail wind during the bike or run? er of these can make the results inaccu- although the reality is that you will not

With planning complete, you are now in a position to take to training.

be able to control the weather on the day of the race and it may have a positive or nega- tive effect on your performance.

It is also very difficult to predict how long you will need to improve your speed across the events. It is generally the case that the longer you have the better, although any period dedicated to this aspect of perform- ance should be rewarded with improved results. At least four weeks devoted to increasing your speed in the three disciplines should produce tangible results. Any longer than twelve weeks focused on this, however, may prove detrimental as the intensity of the training required to deliver results can lead to fatigue, which will have a negative effect on both speed and endurance and force the whole training programme backwards. With this in mind, sufficient rest must be allowed. This should include easy days and complete rest days within the programme, as well as regular easy weeks.

When discussing endurance building we mentioned the possibility of a four- or six-week period of steady solid training followed by an easier week. When the intensity of training is increased to develop a higher overall pace, it is probably prudent to reduce this to two or three weeks of solid harder training with one week of easier training. This will ensure you remain fresh while training and sufficiently rested to complete the necessary workouts, something that is especially important for this kind of training. There is a slightly increased risk of injury when training in this way, which makes it all the more important to give the body suffi-cient time to recuperate and repair itself from the efforts you will be making.

As a novice triathlete approaching the sport for the first time, you should now understand the importance of a planned approach to your training. This is especially important as you are now balancing three sports inside one, and meeting the demands of a sport inside a normal life. We have looked in some detail at how to develop the

necessary endurance base to comple chosen event, what that event may be what the demands of triathlon are in t of potential race distances. I have shown by adopting a two-phase approach to training, building the speed training on of the endurance training, athletes can the goal of achieving a certain time, e now or after their first event. I have looked at what a speed-training progra will involve (this will be investigated in n more detail within the chapters on specific disciplines) and outlined som the other factors you need to consider triathlete, such as nutrition, transition equipment.

Having worked through this cha you should now be in a strong positio start the planning process. Complete basic endurance tests, or possibly the n advanced tests of speed over the discipl Draw up your personal schedule and i tify the training slots that will help you towards being a triathlete. If you comp this to a high standard, it will put well ahead of many of those you mee the start line of your target race. You have taken the first step towards a succe triathlon.

wimming

first discipline in the event, and by far
most technical, swimming presents a real
enge to the novice triathlete. Many
le can swim, and some can swim and
ry competitive, but it requires a special
of skill to swim quickly and then go on
e on a bike and run.

UIPMENT

equipment requirements for swimming
appear to be simple, but proper care
when selecting the right kit for training
acing will enhance the experience in

is probable that the great majority,
all, of your training will be done in
mming pool. If this is the case you
eed a swimming costume. For men
hoice will be between a close-fitting
of swim trunks and more loose-fitting
shorts. A closer fitting garment is the
option as it provides less resistance
vill allow the development of a good
y stroke without the hindrance of
materials. The choice for women
erally between a one- or two-piece
me. Whichever you choose, the cos-
must be comfortable and suitable for
ning rather than sunbathing. A single-
outfit may be right for you, although
are triathlon-specific two-piece cos-
s that are very comfortable and entirely
le.

st swimmers will choose to wear swim-
goggles. There is a huge array of
ent goggle designs and colours and it
ake a bit of experimentation to estab-

lish the best design for you. Goggles should
be comfortable when snugly fitted. How you
care for your goggles, and indeed the other
equipment you use, will play a large part in
determining its longevity. Rinsing all equipment with clean fresh water enhances its
performance and life. The only other equipment you need to add to your costume and
goggles to enable you to start swimming is
a towel, but you might wish to consider a
number of other items. Many people use
some form of footwear when walking around
the swimming pool area, and flip flops can
make the experience much more pleasant
and prevent infections being passed on.

The use of swimming hats is mandatory
in some pools, but may also be advantageous
both for protecting the hair and improving
performance. Swimmers with longer hair
will definitely benefit from using a swimming
hat as this will prevent the distraction caused
by hair moving across the face and inter-
rupting the stroke, as well as providing resistance in the water. Although swim hats are
inexpensive, they too will benefit from the
same level of care as your other equipment.

There are a number of drills and activities
to help you improve your swimming technique and performance. To complete some
of them effectively you may need to use some
form of float, of which there are two basic
types: the pull buoy and the hand float. A
pull buoy is used between the legs to enhance
buoyancy and enable the swimmer to concentrate on the arm function within the
stroke. The hand float can be used in a
number of ways, but is generally employed
to support the upper body when concentrating on improving the leg action.

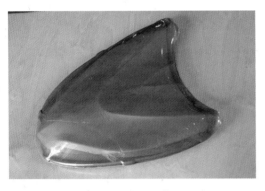

Paddles and flippers can be used in some drills and can enhance the power of a swimmer. They are useful tools, but if a swimmer starts to rely on the sensation that they provide this can have a negative effect on overall swimming performance. If, after reading the information below, you think you will benefit from using these tools, then do so sparingly as part of a balanced programme.

WETSUITS

Many triathlon events take place in water. If you are planning on tac this kind of event you will almost defi need a wetsuit. There are rules relatir the wearing of wetsuits and the maxi swim distance permitted at low and temperatures.

When the temperature is below a ce point it is compulsory to wear a wetsui

Temperature	Max. swim distance
13°C	2,000m
12°C	1,000m
11°C	500m

Wetsuits are not permitted for races a the following temperatures:

Temperature	Swim distance
Above 22°C	< 2,000m
Above 23°C	2,000–2,999m
Above 24°C	> 3,000m

In the UK you are unlikely to be allow start an open water race without a we It is even more unlikely that you will be bidden to wear one owing to high temperature? If you are fortunate enou race abroad then you will need to chec local weather conditions and take a regarding the use of wetsuits.

The selection of a wetsuit is an impc decision. Wetsuits can be hired fr number of companies, allowing the n athlete to take part in an open water without having to commit to the financial purchase of a good quality we If you decide you do want to purch wetsuit, either because you intend to pa pate in a number of events or because have the facility to practice in open v

Facing page: The swim component of triath can generate some impressive images.

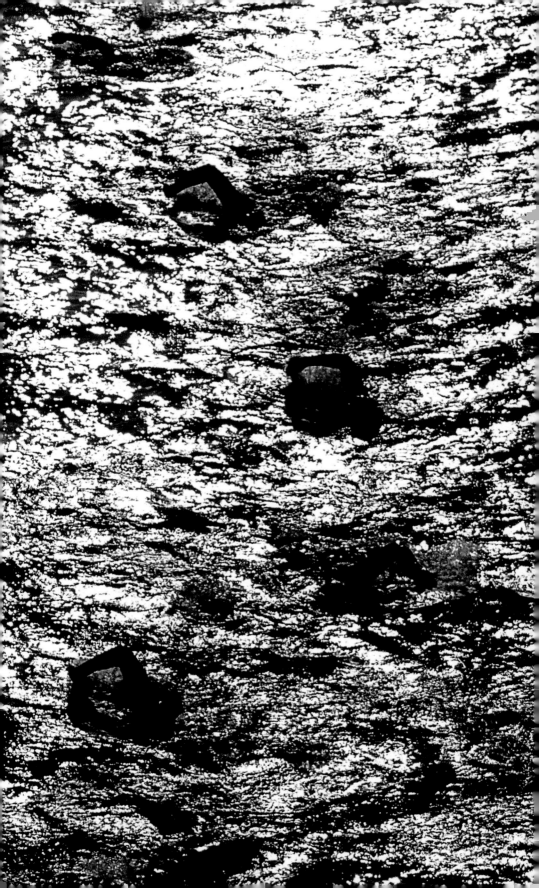

Wetsuits are an unavoidable part of triathlon in the UK.

then you will need some guidance. Triathlon magazines such as *220 Triathlon* carry a wide variety of advertisements for triathlon-specific wetsuits. These have been designed specifically for the demands of the sport and are cut appropriately around the arms to allow flexibility in a way not often found in those designed for diving, skiing or generic water sports. This is not to say you cannot use these suits, but they may not be as comfortable and the experience may not be as pleasant.

SWIMMING TECHNIQUE AND THEORY

The three most important things to becoming a successful swimmer are: technique, technique and technique.

Of the three disciplines, swimming is by far the most technically difficult to master. This is largely because, as land-based animals, we were not given the characteristics of fish. The medium in which the action takes place (water) is unforgiving, principally because it is nearly one thousand times denser than air. The harder you hit it the harder it hits you

back. The swimmer should understand an increase in swim speed results i increase in resistance This in turn means an increase in effort can be counterpro tive if not coupled with good techn Newcomers to the sport, or athletes have a background in either runnin cycling, seldom find it easy to adapt t demands of swimming for these reason

Competitive swimming requires the a to be metronomic, and the swimmer h be trained to control and maintain ce variables under race pressure. Swimmi an objective sport with races decided by is fastest from point A to point B or, often, the fastest time over a set dista The most successful swimmers are al robotic and are able constantly to mai their technique and maximize propu movements, while at the same time r mizing resistive forces acting against body. The ability to slip, slide and through the water in a seemingly re manner is paramount. The swimmer sh understand that physical conditioning a the swimmer to apply propulsive force reduce resistive force for longer period more efficiently, but technique is a lim factor in performance. Novice triath

it difficult at times to understand that
ovements in swimming do not result
 more hours of physical work in the
. Cyclists and runners are used to making
 physical efforts to improve their per-
ance on the road or track. However,
does not necessarily apply to the pool.
 basic fundamentals required for good
nique will be discussed below.
very swimmer is faced with the challenge
nted by his physical characteristics,
 as flexibility, limb length, strength
body shape. How a swimmer propels
ody through the water is a complex
ct and various scientific theories on
ulsion are still being explored. One thing
tain, though: in order to move forward
ater you have to apply force. When
ing a propulsive force to a low viscosity
 (water), you will move some of this

Preparing for a swim start can be a nervous
time.

Good technique and practice is essential for any
triathlon, especially a mass start event.

fluid in the opposite direction to the direction of motion. This was once thought to be the way to move forwards in water – to move forwards you push water back. Newton's third law of motion, which states that 'any action has an equal and opposite reaction', would seem to support this type of propulsive effort. However, it is not quite that simple. If a swimmer pushes his or her hand straight backwards (without the sweeping action), a considerable mass of water moving with it has a negative effect on the propulsive force (forward motion).

Swimmers actually move more effectively through the water by making sculling or sweeping (curved line path) movements with their hands. By changing the path of their hand during the propulsive movement, a smaller mass of water is moved as the hand searches for 'still' water. The use of the hand in curved sweeping movements allows the swimmer to use 'lift' forces to create propulsion and forward movement.

Swimmers curve/cup their hands, and the water that moves over the back of the hand moves faster than the water at the front when the swimmer is applying pressure. There is a corresponding decrease in pressure at the back of the hand. Objects tend to move from areas of higher to lower pressure and so a lift force is created.

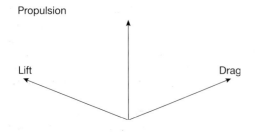

Swimmers use this 'lift' force to create forward movement by using their hands like rotating propellers as they sweep their hands through the water, creating lift and so propulsion. The complex subject of propulsion in water is further complicated by the individual variation of hand pitch, angle of attack and velocity. It is almost impossible

The arm recovers above the water.

to predict the ideal stroke pattern for swimmer. However, in order to pro effective propulsion the swimmer sh practise:

- *A good 'catch' point*. This is where pre sion through the water begins. The enters the water smoothly and trav short distance forward under the before the hand will 'catch'. The starts to feel against the resistance o water and then pull against it, movin hand and arm underneath the head body. It is important not to start pulling action too quickly, but to with the fingers and have a firm This allows the hand to feel for the sure of the water

- *High elbow position*: The hand stays the elbow moves over the hand as shoulder rotates, allowing the swim to skull their hand laterally and verti The high elbow position ensures t correct position is held throughout action and is more a symptom of technique than a cause. It must ther be combined with all the other as discussed here

- *'S' pulls*: Lots of sculling drills while hand is moving through the water ene ages holding the 'pressure' throug the propulsive effort and therefore g ates a forward movement. This is e

- *Wave drag*: caused by the waves swimmers make as they move through the water and the action of the waves against the swimmer
- *Frictional drag*: friction between the body and swimwear and the surrounding water molecules
- *Eddy currents*: the tendency of water to fill in behind the swimmer as the body moves forwards, therefore generating a drag to pull the swimmer backwards with the moving water

In order to reduce drag to a minimum, the swimmer needs to present as little frontal mass to the water as possible. Effective streamlining is essential. The coach should train swimmers to swim in two straight lines:

- A horizontal line from head to feet is desirable: the straighter this line, the less form drag and wave drag is generated
- A vertical line from head to feet, when the swimmer is viewed from behind or above, is also desirable

Any movement of the body from side to side will increase form drag, wave drag and eddy currents. Because of the relativly slow speed of swimming, frictional drag is not as critical. Using a triathlon-specific wetsuit and a swim hat will probably be enough to help you reduce fictional drag. Some races use a personal timing chip issued to each swimmer to help with collating accurate results. This is often placed around the ankle on a strap, but careful positioning can help ensure that it is neither uncomfortable nor presenting too much drag.

The shape and orientation of the body in the water determines how much resistance will be encountered – the more tapered and slender the shape the better. A tapered shape disrupts the water less, presents less frontal mass and allows water molecules to fill in almost immediately after the body passes thought the water. Fish obviously have the ideal shape for moving through water. In comparison, however, the human body shape is poorly designed for this purpose. Furthermore, swimmers change position

olside observer or coach will be able to spot with your stroke.

scribed as an 'S' pull, as the hand and m track an elongated S through the ter

celeration: Start each pull with the hand d arm through the water slowly, at st feeling for the pressure and then celerating through the propulsive pull-g phase until the hand and arm exit the ter

hape of the human body is not designed ove through water. While it may look we swim on the surface, we actually through the surface of the water. The ntial for negative resistant force (drag) tremely high. Four types of drag hold wimmer back:

rm drag: caused by the size and shape the body as it is presented to the ter

Swimmers displaying good positioning and holding line in water well.

constantly as they swim, presenting a variety of shapes to oncoming water flow.

The swimmer's objective is to reduce these variations to an absolute minimum and eliminate any unnecessary movement.

When swimmers increase speed they create more turbulence and increase their drag. The faster they swim, the more resistance they create. Speed in water is governed by what is known as the Theoretical Square Law. An athlete swimming three times as fast does not create just three times as much resistance; instead he will actually create a square of his swim speed, resulting in nine times as much resistance. Technique and streamlining help to reduce drag as speed increases and good pace will leave the swimmer with more energy to overcome drag towards the end of the swim section and throughout the rest of the triathlon.

FRONT CRAWL TECHNIQUES

Front crawl is the fastest of the four competitive strokes and is the most energy efficient. This makes it the stroke recommended for overall conditioning is an essential skill for triathletes, speed and energy efficiency are importa multi-sport events. With this stroke, the is directed backwards and there is con uous propulsion. Being better stream than any other, the stroke is highly effic particularly for long-distance events suc the IRONMAN. The following descrip is not a definitive explanation of the st but rather a guide to the basic fundame required to swim the stroke at a compe level.

Body position

The body should be as flat, horizo and streamlined as possible, just below surface. The head should be in line the body, in a relatively natural position is, not lifted or looking down), with the looking diagonally forward and down, angle of about 45 degrees, and the v breaking the forehead just above eyel level. It is essential that the head sh

*: Swimming in public, sometimes very
in public, is part of triathlon.

Below: Pool swim events are particularly useful for
building the confidence of less able swimmers.

A good example of well-executed breathing.

remain still and central during the stroke cycle. To prevent excess turbulence, except when breathing, the shoulders and hips should be high in the water, with the feet just below the surface. Rotation around the long axis is required to allow effective propulsive movements of the arms and legs and to facilitate breathing action.

It is important to encourage full rotation of the body so that the hips and shoulders roll together and the swimmer avoids the problem known as 'fixed' hips. Correct body rolling technique can make the front crawl action much more streamlined and efficient. This rolling motion not only makes the stroke look more effortless, but it actually does make it easier to perform. The body must be kept horizontal in the water as much as possible when viewed from the side, and a vertical/straight line when viewed from above or behind.

Leg action

Leg action and head position are two of the fundamental components to an effective body position in the water. The main role o leg action is to balance the propulsive n ments of the arms and maintain a str lined body position. Different variatio the kick are possible, for example two- four-beat and six-beat, where the figure r to the number of times the legs are ki for every stroke the arms perform. Swim will almost always naturally use the kick is best suited to them. Triathletes who pete in sprint distance events tend to fa a higher beat leg kick, while Ironman petitors tend to adopt a two- or four-kick owing to the reduced energy costs as ated with them. Ankle flexibility is of importance to the effectiveness of the for both propulsion and balance. Alth many triathletes believe that the kick is an important component of the strok swimming in triathlon, this is not true. kick plays a major role in maintaining a rect body position and the use of the le essential. It is true that when using a w the legs will naturally be more buoyant this must not be relied upon and a g efficient kick is still necessary.

ing a good
ht position in a
swim.

wnbeat: The kick is initiated from the
ps and the thigh and is swept down-
ards as the foot passes the hips during
e previous upbeat. The knee and ankle
ints should be relaxed with the foot held
a planter-flexed position. The whip-like
tion towards the end of the downbeat
sults in the legs snapping straight. This
tion brings the largest area of the feet in
ntact with the water pressure in a back-
ards and downwards direction. Some
toeing can occur during this phase

• *Upbeat*: The leg should be extended and straight, with the foot in a slightly dorsi-flex position so that it rebounds upwards as the previous downbeat is completed. The thigh initiates the upkick and the knee flexes slightly. The foot is planter flexed before the start of the downbeat. A good coaching tip is to keep the leg fairly straight on the upbeat to avoid excessive bending of the knees. The kick should be maintained within the body depth (about 30–45cm). If this range is

Propulsion from legs is
still very important for
triathlon swimmers.

A leg action seen from above, with heels close to the surface but not breaking.

extended, then unnecessary resistance can occur

- *Limb path*: It is important that the kick is not entirely on a vertical plane but rather that it moves with the hip rotation created by the body roll. The kick will move through a diagonal and vertical direction

Arm action

The main propulsive force of the front crawl is derived from the arms, which employ an alternating action with continuous movement. The hand enters in front of the head and in line with the shoulder. It should be about halfway between the shoulder and fully extended arm stretch. The hand should be angled at approximately 35 degrees with a clean thumb first entry. The hand is extended forwards just below the water surface to full extension but without overreaching.

- *Downsweep*: The hand sculls outw and downwards to the catch point. hand resists the pressure of the w and the shoulder rotates medially to the elbow (high elbow). The hand continues to sweep outwards and do wards
- *Insweep*: The elbow increases in fle and the pitch of the hand turns inw The hand sweeps inwards and acce tion of the hand increases
- *Upsweep*: The hand pitch adjusts aga a backward and outward position. fingers point down until the final st as the hand sweeps up, out and b Acceleration continues. When the h passes the hips, the wrist rotates releases the water. The hand is no position for exit
- *Sweeping movement*: When viewed f below, the hand should follow the

ape pull pattern. The severity of the 'S'
ll depend on individual characteristics,
ch as strength

covery: This should be made with high
ows and no tension in the hands or
ns. The fingers should point down and
e hand should start to reach for entry
ce the arm passes the head

thing

hing in swimming has to be taught
can be quite challenging for the non-
mer to master. The head should rotate
ally as the arm is pulled back. Breathing
d be at the end of the propulsive phase

provide most of the propulsion.

of the arm, with the head as low as possible.
In fact the swimmer should breathe in the
bow wave created by the head.

The head should turn at approximately
45 degrees to the side, so that the swimmer is looking at the poolside wall, and
return smoothly and without delay following
breathing. The face should be back in the
water before the arm passes the head during
the recovery phase. Bilateral breathing should
be encouraged even if the swimmer does not
use it in a race, since the ability to breathe
to both sides is very important and will
remove a potential handicap. If a swimmer
is capable of breathing only to one side, they
may be at a disadvantage in open water if

Open water technique is basically the same as pool swimming.

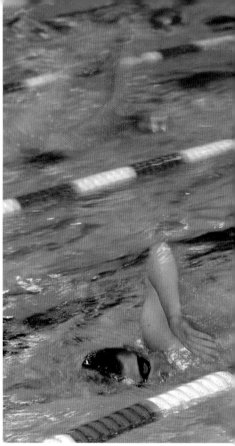

A swimmer demonstrates a good recovery.

Swimmer in centre shot prepares for hand entry.

how the swimmer's hand exits the water in a very
style.

vind or waves are coming from that
tion. In this situation the ability to
he to the other side will be invaluable,
so a proportion of training should be
in this fashion. Bilateral breathing
urages the return of the head to the
al position and is good for stroke
ce and control. The swimmer should
he out gradually underwater with full
exhalation at the end of the pulling phase of
the arm.

Timing

Different timings of the kick to the arms may
be employed: two-beat, four-beat, six-beat
and two-beat crossover kicks. The six-
beat kick is generally more propulsive but

Good example of
breathing in the wake
of a stroke.

Open water move off from a boom.

also uses more energy; many distance swim-mers swim with reduced kicks and then increase the kick rate towards the end of a race. The important thing with kicking and timing is that it must balance the arm stroke and keep the body in straight alignment so that less resistance is created. Whatever timing is used, the kick should balance the sweeping action of the arm.

TRAINING

Tips for freestyle

Good kicking ability is important when swimming freestyle. A good strong kick improves stroke balance. The legs have to be extremely conditioned as they work hard throughout the entire race distance. If the legs fatigue too early in the race, stroke balance is lost and resistance is increased. To help prevent this, do some of your training using a hand float, so that all the propu comes from your legs alone.

Hand paddles are excellent for impro technique and developing strength and muscular endurance in the upper body. should be only slightly larger than the su area of the individual's hand. Care sh be taken when using paddles to prevent straining.

All swimmers, even distance swimm need speed. For this reason swimmin improve speed should be included w your practice time. Short bursts at maxi speed over distances of approximately 25m are best.

Core strength is vital in freestyle s ming, where effective energy transf required through the body. For this re swimmers should do regular abdominal lower back strength exercises.

Freestyle swimmers need to work o ability to use bilateral breathing. In tria

useful to look both ways and be aware
e competition. The main advantage of
ral breathing is that it helps to balance
stroke, as the head always returns to
centre while the body is encouraged
rform full body roll on both breathing
non-breathing sides. Furthermore, it
ces the possibility of developing muscle
lances, which can be associated with
teral breathing (breathing to one side

hen training using the freestyle stroke
n endurance type event, and once they
apable of covering the race distance
are confident with this distance, swim-
should perform a high-intensity over-
ace set (more than the race distance) at
twice a month.
durance should always be developed
The introduction of higher intensity
peed should follow once endurance has
developed. This will usually occur
g the months leading up to the target

water swimming can create
a splash.

Always train for the race model, taking
into consideration stroke count, stroke rate,
pace and tactics. If you are required to start
fast in a triathlon event and then settle onto
a steady pace, you should practise this in
training sets.

Try to include variety into your sessions.
Do not swim the same session every time
you go to the pool. Different strokes provide
variety and are good for skill application and
recovery. Back-stroke is particularly good as
a recovering stroke after freestyle sets.

Remember that active rest will improve
recovery rate. Always incorporate gentle
swimming between hard training efforts to
aid recovery.

Do some sets that require a sustained
effort for at least the duration of the race.
These are more beneficial for endurance
athletes than descending sets.

During training consistently stress the 3-
Rs: Range (length of stroke); Rhythm (good
cadence); and Relaxation (smooth, relaxed
action).

Drills carried out in a pool environment are better with training partners.

Front crawl skill development drills

Swimmers should always endeavour to swim with perfect technique in training so that the correct movement pattern becomes in-grained. A drill is simply a concerted and concentrated effort on one specific compon-ent of the swimming stroke. Drills are vital to help isolate particular skills. If correctly performed they will have a beneficial transfer effect to the full stroke. Here are some key drills to develop front crawl:

- *Kicking drills*: The kick can be performed with a kick board using 'deep' and 'shallow' kicking techniques. This im-proves the feel for the water pressure on the feet. The kick can also be performed on the front, back and side without a board and with good streamlining.

Drills prepare us for race day. All top triathletes, such as Jodie Swallow, will have completed many hours of drills.

rtical kicking in deep water with the nds out is also good for testing kick iciency and developing kick power and ength

per slow swimming: Performance of the l stroke in slow motion without pause quires concentration and control. The immer has to balance and stabilize, and n 'feel' stroke patterns and problems. is is an excellent method of refining e front crawl stroke

tch-up freestyle: For this particular drill, e hand stays in front of the head at the tch position. The swimmer does not pull at hand back until the other has reached e front of the stroke and both hands e side by side. This is a very effective ill for teaching full extension of the arm d stroke length

ickle freestyle: The swimmer swims nor- ally but has to trail the finger tips in the ter during recovery phase of the arm stroke. This is a particularly good drill for teaching high elbow recovery and encour- aging body roll

- *Head-up freestyle*: The swimmer performs the normal freestyle stroke but with the head up. This is good for working on the entry position of the hands and the slide forward to catch. A 'high' elbow is essen- tial and the swimmer can check entry and elbow position during the swim

- *Fist swimming*: Swimming with the hands closed takes away the effects of using the 'paddle'. When alternated with normal hand position, the swimmer is reminded to hold the pressure on the hands and emphasize pulling with the arms. This par- ticular drill can be used to develop the execution of the power phase in a straight line and corrects any glide away of the hands after entry

- *Single-arm swimming*: The arm on the non-breathing side is extended and held

swimmers need to swim freestyle with heads up so hey can sight during an open water swim.

in front. This allows the swimmer to work on the breathing side of the stroke. This drill encourages a good turn of the head when breathing, enabling the swimmer and coach to check the timing of the head turn relative to the arm stroke on the breathing side. A kick board can be used in the outstretched arm to aid support and balance, so making it possible to concentrate fully on the breathing and the stroke cycle

• *Using fins*: All swimmers should have a pair of fins. They should not be too long – top swimmers often cut them down to size. Fins are good for improving ankle flexibility and generally offer support when performing drills. This extra support enables the swimmer to concentrate on the training requirements of the drill. However, the swimmer should not become dependent on the fin: always alternate technique work with and without fins. Speed work with fins is also beneficial since they enable the swimmer to move faster than their race pace and so provide muscular contractions at speed, which is good for the central nervous system and muscle fibre recruitment

SWIM TRAINING PRINCIPLES

Physical conditioning in swimming is no different to that required by many sports. The best results in performance will be obtained by following the recognized principles of training. In the context of triathlon, swimming is essentially an endurance-based sport. Cardiovascular fitness and local muscular endurance are key to optimal performance. This is not to say other aspects of fitness, such as strength, power and flexibility, are not important but rather that endurance should be the foundation on which the other components of fitness are built.

Physical stress

Physical stress is not bad for you. In fact, it is actually very good for you, so long as it is applied at the right level and frequency.

It provides the body with the stimulu positive change. Judgement of the inte duration and frequency of physical that the swimmer should undergo thr the training programme lies at the he the coach's trade.

Adaptation

Adaptation is the term given to how body copes with the training stress ap The body will change or adapt so that better able to cope with the stress next it is applied. If the stress is applied co ently, in the correct manner, the body adapt in a positive long-term fashion. T ing effects such as improved cardiovas endurance, lower resting heart rate, imp stroke volume and increased cardiac o are all examples of long-term adaptatio

Recovery

Rest or recovery is an essential compone well-planned training programmes. A tation cannot take place if the swimm over-trained or stressed too often or a high an intensity without sufficient rec periods. Adaptation takes place during pe of rest or reduced intensity.

Overload

For a swimmer to improve continually necessary to incorporate overload into ing programmes. Once the swimmer re a certain level of fitness on a certain of training they will stay at that point stress must increase to provide stimulu further adaptation. Overload can be incr in a variety of ways, including introdu increases in training hours, volume, inte or duration, and by allowing less rest bet repeats. However, the most effective w see further improvements is to increas swimming speed for a given training set

Progression

Overload must be applied progressively planned and coordinated way. This co essential component of the process of ovement, and must be considered when ning training sessions. Too much over- too soon, will lead to an inability to t. If this inappropriate overload con- s through poor training and competi- results, failing adaptation can be the rsor of over-training and eventual s. Progression and overload should be natically planned into the training pro- me to maximize adaptation.

ificity

get what you train for.' Swimmers ld place demands on themselves in ng that will prepare them for the inten- nd duration of the event in which they ete. This is not to say that every train- ession should be at race pace, but the rements of the race should be system- ly prepared for throughout a number aining sessions. It is important to mber that in triathlon you will get only ited transfer of fitness components from discipline to another. The best way to re to swim fast is to do it in the pool.

Reversibility

'If you don't use it, you lose it'. This is par- ticularly true of swimming, in which mus- cular endurance is best achieved by swim training. You may increase cardiovascular endurance by cycling or running, but if you lose muscular endurance by not doing reg- ular pool sessions you will not be able to use your cardiovascular endurance, since the arms and legs will fatigue first during competition.

INTERVAL TRAINING

DIRT principles

When constructing swimming training sets, the following variables should be used and controlled:

D = Distance, e.g. 100m, 200m, 400m

I = Interval of rest – always use a turn-
   around time in preference to rest
   interval, so that you can control the
   speed of the swim and the amount of
   rest

ng around a buoy is a swim skill exclusive to triathlon.

Designing a swimming training programme by DIRT principles			
	January	*March*	*May*
D =	100m	100m	100m
I =	@ 90 seconds	@ 85 seconds	@ 85 seconds
R =	× 20	× 20	× 20
T =	Hold 69 seconds	Hold 67 seconds	Hold 65 second

R = Number of repetitions, e.g. 20, 30, 40

T = Time – a target for each repetition. This is obviously related to intensity and swim speed and should be based on the personal best time of the swimmer for a given distance. The closer the swimmer swims to their personal best times, the more demanding the intensity. The further away from the best time, the easier the intensity. The important thing to remember is that, by asking the swimmer to repeat the time, the coach is controlling the effort of the swim.

By controlling these variables, training sessions can be produced that give control over volume, duration, intensity, rest and speed. The sets are measurable and can be logged and evaluated by both the swimmer and the coach. This type of set construction lends itself to the application of training overload and progression.

Designing training sets

Once you are familiar with the DIRT principles of training variables, it is relatively simple to alter each component to achieve a desired physiological training effect. Most physiologists agree on the six main training areas suitable for manipulation:

• Endurance maintenance
• Endurance overload
• Lactate threshold training
• Lactate production

• Lactate tolerance
• Sprint speed

The training target is obviously relate the event. Sprinters, for example, sh do more anaerobic and speed work wit endurance-based training. Endurance-l athletes should do a higher percenta; aerobic endurance and lactate threshold work, with less emphasis on speed and a obic work.

When an individual starts to exercis anaerobic energy system is recruited The main source of energy for this syst Phosphocreatine (PCr). Its effect is im iate but short-lived, lasting for only a ten seconds. During this time the body not actually require any oxygen, henc term anaerobic. Since neither lactic acic carbon dioxide is produced as a v product, it is also termed alactic.

The glycolytic system, which is the se system to be recruited, is not as short as that derived from PCr, since it cal for up to 60 or 70 seconds. Like the system, the glycolytic system is anaer but it does produce lactic acid as a v product. A 400m runner, for example be recruiting the PCr and much of the g lytic system during the course of a rac that by the time they cross the finishin; the lactic acid levels in the muscles w very high and will be burning.

Throughout these two anaerobic s the body is operating without oxygen a burning only carbohydrate as a fuel, lactic acid as the waste product.

If we move along this time continut

nt between 60 and 90 seconds, the next n to be recruited is the aerobic system. is when your body can produce vast nts of adenosine triphosphate (ATP) ically to deliver sufficient oxygen to n your level of work. Build up of lactic is minimal. Both fat and carbohydrate sed as fuel, although at this stage there greater reliance on fat than on carbo- te. This system is very slow in compar- to the other two systems, and has a slow ver of energy production, which is why hlete is able to work for a prolonged d of time using this system.

the intensity of exercise increases the moves through the aerobic system to naerobic. It is worth remembering this being aware that increases in intensity rely on different methods of produc- nergy and propelling the body. A term ently used is threshold. This refers to imit of aerobic capacity or the highest sity you can sustain before your body s to use the anaerobic energy system. is important as the higher the intensity an sustain without relying on the anaer- systems the more efficient you will be he faster you can go for longer, which ghly desirable for swimming, cycling, ng and, of course, triathlon.

ith the knowledge of the energy sys- we can now analyse potential training ns. The following are examples of the ent criteria coaches have used when iling swimming training sets.

ria for endurance maintenance set truction
distance: 2,000–8,000m or 20–90 nutes
peat distances: any can be used ensity: Light; short rest intervals (5–30 conds)
ced: Approximately 3–4 seconds per 0m slower than threshold endurance

ria for endurance overload set truction
distance: 1,500–2,000m or 20–25 nutes
peat distance: 100–1,500m

- Rest interval: 30–90 seconds
- Speed: 2 seconds per 100m faster than endurance threshold; fastest possible average throughout the set

Criteria for lactate threshold endurance set construction
- Set distance: 2,000–3,000 or 25–40 minutes
- Repeat distance: 25–3,000m
- Rest intervals: 10–30 seconds
- Speed: at individual 'anaerobic threshold'
- Intensity: Maximum even pace for the duration of the set (25–40 minutes)

Criteria for lactic production set construction
- Set distance: 200–500m per set (1–3 sets per training session)
- Repeat distance: 25–75m
- Rest intervals: 1–4 minutes
- Speed: as fast as possible (~ 98 per cent of season's best time)
- Intensity: Maximum
- Suggested total distance per week: 1,000–3,000m, depending on cycle stage

Criteria for sprint speed set construction
- Set distance: 200–300m per set (1–2 sets per training session)
- Repeat distances: 10–50m (including starts and turns)
- Rest intervals: 30 seconds–5 minutes
- Speed: maximum and faster than race pace

KEEPING YOUR BALANCE

Top competitive swimmers can train for anything up to twenty-six hours per week in the pool, and cover training volumes in excess of 80km during this time. The triathlete, however, must balance swim training with other disciplines. Many factors will decide this balance. How good is your swimming ability? Is it strong or weak? These are matters for you and possibly your coach to decide. It is important to use swim sessions to complement running and cycling sessions and vice versa. Remember, the principles of

Balance your swim training with the other disciplines to prevent injury.

training apply no matter what training is taking place. It would be unwise to perform a high-intensity workout in the pool followed by a workout of similar intensity for running or cycling. With careful planning, sessions can be integrated. For example, you may wish to do some power work on the bike and then some steady kick work in the pool to aid recovery of the legs. Or you may do a hard muscular endurance pool session on the arms in the pool and then follow this with an endurance run on the legs after the swim session. The main thing is to get the correct balance of training intensity, regardless of which discipline you are training on, and allow for adequate rest to achieve maximum adaptation.

DEVELOPING YOUR STROKE

Stroke efficiency

The swimmer needs to ingrain into memory a stroke that will be effic and repeatable under pressure. An effic technique will generate maximum f during propulsive movements with mir energy requirements and minimum re ance. Stroke efficiency requires years of stant attention to detail and control v training. Great swimmers are able to s at fast speeds with relatively few str because they can 'fix' on the water and pr their body past the fixed point.

Superior technique also gives them resistance. These two factors allow t to get maximum distance per stroke (D Efficiency is a combination of DPS, length of stroke, how many strokes a sw mer takes for a given speed and the spee the stroke cycles.

Stroke counting

Each swimmer has an optimal stroke c for a race. It is individual and compari with other swimmers cannot be made. aim is to swim at a predetermined sp with the minimum number of stro A reduction in stroke count at the s swim speed, or faster, indicates an impr ment in stroke efficiency. For exan if a swimmer can swim 400m freestyle minutes 30 seconds with 60 strokes/1 in the early season and then swims 4 min 30 seconds with 56 strokes/100m late the season, then they have improved st efficiency by swimming the same speed less energy expenditure. The critical fa are time and speed. Anyone can take f strokes and swim slowly. The target maintain or increase swim speed with f strokes. It would be tedious to attemp count all strokes on every lap in training with some thought a control method ca introduced to training:

20 × 100m freestyle with 20 rest
Hold 28 strokes/50m
Hold 75 seconds swim time

...ke rate

...e rate is the speed of the stroke cycles
...swimmer's turnover rate. This is also
...n as cadence. Again it is individual and
...swimmer will have an optimal stroke
...If your stroke rate is too fast you lose
...'fix on the water' and 'spin', resulting
...or propulsion that wastes much energy.
...oke rate that is too slow will prevent
...rom swimming at the optimum speed,
...se you do not generate enough force-
...ropulsive movements. Swimmers and
...es should experiment with different
...until the individual optimum rate is
...1. This rate should then be ingrained
...training. Again, the stroke rate should
...ounted during races. As swimmers be-
...tired they cannot maintain their speed
...oke and their rate will drop. Experi-
...1 competitive swimmers, however, can
...a set rate during the race and increase
...vards the finish.

...ke length

...rally speaking, the longer the length of
...e the better. This should not be con-
...with 'over reaching' in front crawl,
...1 is actually a fault. Stroke length is the
...xtension of the arm at the front and
...oack of each propulsive movement:
...onger the stroke length, the longer the
...ct with the water during the propulsive
...: and the greater the potential for the
...cation of force. Swimmers lose stroke
...h when they grow tired and try to com-
...te with an increase in stroke count.

...nce per stroke

...nce per stroke is the distance travelled
...ch arm stroke. All great swimmers are
...o travel large distances with few strokes.
...nce per stroke is an indication of effi-
...y. It requires good stroke length and
...bility to 'fix' on the water. Technique
...portant so that the arm is in the best
...on mechanically to generate force,
...resistance from the rest of the body is
...nized.

Maintenance of stroke efficiency and the importance of pace

Fatigue will have a detrimental effect on the stroke count, stroke rate, stroke length and distance per stroke. The classic signs of fatigue in races are an increased stroke count, loss of stroke rate and stroke length, and a corresponding reduction in distance per stroke. If the stroke falls apart like this, efficiency is low and as a consequence energy expenditure will be high. Swimmers need to train to pace themselves correctly so that extreme fatigue is experienced only towards the end of the race. Swimmers also have to be trained to maintain optimum stroke count, stroke rate, stroke length and distance per stroke under race pressure. Most swimmers prefer to swim endurance races (400m and upwards) in an evenly paced fashion. Each segment of the race is performed in the same time with effort increasing toward the finish, for example:

400m freestyle – final time
4 minutes 40 seconds
Split each 100m: 70, 70, 70, 70 seconds

Another method is to 'negative split' the race. Here the swimmer would swim the second half of the race faster than the first half, for example:

400m freestyle – final time
4 minutes 38 seconds
Split each 100m: 70, 70, 70, 68 seconds

The advantage of this type of pace is that it allows the swimmer to use the available energy over the race distance without a build up of lactic acid until the closing stages. It also allows the swimmer to settle into an optimum stroke count, stroke rate, stroke length and distance per stroke, and maintain this during the race distance.

OPEN WATER

There are a number of specific skills required to swim in an open water competition.

Open water starting can be particularly challenging for swimmers who are only used to pool swimming.

In most events the start will be from a stationary position, but in deep water. This means you must be able to tread water and then move into your stroke. This is something that does not come easily to swimmers who have only ever used the side of a pool to kick off from, so practise treading water and then moving into your stroke. The start of any open water triathlon can be a little frantic. While most races will start you in relatively small groups, the experience of starting with a number of swimmers very close to you can be unnerving. Many first-time triathletes can be drawn into swimming much faster than they want to, with the effort taking its toll in the later stages of the swim or triathlon. Do not be afraid to start off steadily and work your way up to speed as the initial surge forward will relax as the swim progresses.

You will need to be able to navigate as there are no lines to follow in open water

events. Wherever possible you shoul[d] looking to find a buoy that marks the c[...] or the lead boat, which is often a can[...] this is not possible you will need to lo[...] sights on the bank of the water. The [...] nique of sighting is one that must be [...] tised as it can be very disruptive to the [...] stroke. You need to maintain forward m[...] but also look up and forward as you [...] plete your breathing to the side. This c[...] practised in a pool and will provide [...] feeling of doing this during a stroke.

The ability to turn while swimm[...] without using a wall to push off, also [...] to be practised. This can be done by s[...] turning in the pool before you reach [...] wall. Since you will not generally swi[...] an out and back course, however, it is [...] portant to practise how to turn at [...] angles. This is to ensure that you can f[...] the course around buoys when racing in [...] water.

Rules of triathlon: swimming

essential that you are aware of the competition rules that apply to each discipline in triathlon.
following rules are as detailed by the British Triathlon Association, although they broadly
y also to International Triathlon Union races and Ironman races.

1 Competitors shall use no aids other than a cap, goggles, nose clip and a costume, which
    may be a wetsuit

2 A wetsuit may consist of up to three separate parts. The wearing of wetsuit leggings only,
    gloves and/or socks is not permitted. The maximum permitted thickness of material is
    5mm. This maximum thickness also applies to any overlap of material/s

3 The minimum temperature at which wetsuits are optional is 14°C

4 At the following temperatures the following maximum swim distances are obligatory:

Temperature	Max. distance
13°C	2,000m
12°C	1,000m
11°C	500m

Note: Based on the above table, the minimum temperature for a standard distance swim
(1,500m) is 12.5°C

5 At temperatures less than 11°C it is recommended that no open water swimming take
    place. The above are based on water temperatures alone and assume that the wind chill
    factor is negligible. If wind chill is significant, swim distances may be reduced at higher
    temperatures

6 The use of wetsuits is forbidden if the following combinations of distance and water tem-
    perature are attained:

Temperature	Max. distance
> 21°C	< 2,000m
> 22°C	2,000–2,999m
> 23°C	3,000m +

Swim safety – open water

1 Straight line courses: Safety craft or platforms shall be stationed at 100m intervals along
    the course spaced from the back marker to 200m in front of the lead swimmer. Additional
    boats/canoes shall patrol the swimming area to ensure that no swimmer is at any time
    more than 50m from safety cover

2 Circuit courses: Safety craft shall be spaced at 100m intervals with canoe, boat or lifeguard
    backup so as to achieve a ratio of one safety unit per 20 swimmers. At no time should any
    swimmer be more than 50m from safety cover

Rules of triathlon: swimming *continued*

10.3 No safety cover shall leave the course or be withdrawn until the last swimmer has left water

10.4 A suitable craft shall act as guide by maintaining station 25m in front of the leading m and female swimmers

10.5 All turns shall be clearly marked by buoys or other forms of marking. These must be least 1m high

10.6 The course shall be clearly marked by buoys or other marking devices located at le every 100m and a minimum of 1m high. All markers shall be a different colour to sw hats

10.7 First aid units in attendance must be aware of the requirements for the treatment of sh and cold

10.8 Sufficient blankets should be on hand to supply a minimum of 20 per cent of the entr

10.9 Re-heat facilities are to be on hand, together with a good supply of hot drinks

10.10 Water temperature should be measured at a minimum of three points along the cou including the mid and furthest points from the shore, at a depth of 50cm. The low measured temperature should be considered the official water temperature. Temperat readings should be taken within one hour of the start of the event and announced at le 30 minutes before the start of the race

10.11 Wherever practical the ratio of the sections should be maintained when the swimming tance is reduced

10.12 The nearest hospital casualty department must be informed that any race with an op water swim is taking place. Details given must include event location, start time a numbers of competitors expected

DESIGNING YOUR SWIM TRAINING PROGRAMME

So far we have looked at the technical aspects of swimming and at some of the sessions you may use to develop specific components of fitness. Following what you have read so far, you should now start to understand what the swim training programme for triathlon will look like. The idea is to build up your endurance by using the 10 per cent rule, at the same time mastering a good swim stroke for triathlon. Take note of the various criteria that should be observed so that your training sessions develop the necessary c ponents of fitness. Also make sure you aware of the special skills needed to comp in an open water triathlon.

You should now take the time to plar content and targets of your training sessi Look at the time planner you compl and highlight when you will be going sw ming. Drawing on the data from your l endurance and speed tests, set your ol tives for these sessions. This may be as sir as increasing the endurance and distanc a set amount, or practising a specific comp ent of the stroke. Without these objec vill simply be going for a swim rather training.

ice swimming is much more technical the other two disciplines, there is the complication that you have to refine stroke before you can increase endurand speed. Follow the description above component parts of a good stroke and experienced swimmers carefully to an appreciation of the smooth unhurtyle of a good swimmer. It can be very ult, however, to get any real idea of swimming style without the advice raining partner, friend or coach. Ask to watch you carefully or, better still, the action of your stroke so that

together you can compare it with the ideal, so establishing your strengths and weaknesses. You should spend at least half of your swim training time working on improving your technique and the rest building up your endurance and speed in the way described in Chapter 1. Building in this way will ensure that good technique is ingrained throughout your swimming.

We have, of course, assumed that you can swim basic front crawl. Any would-be triathlete without even a basic front crawl stroke should seek the advice of a swimming teacher; details of suitably qualified individuals may be found at local leisure centres.

CHAPTER 3
Cycling

Most people have ridden a bike at some point in their lives, but refining the skills and techniques of bike riding will vastly improve triathlon performance regardless of the type of bike you are riding. This chapter is concerned with ensuring you adopt good bike-handling skills and an economical cycling position, and developing your speed and endurance so that you can achieve all goals.

CYCLING EQUIPMENT

Cycling is the only triathlon discipline that is heavily reliant on equipment. As part of this module we will look closely at the issues of equipment selection and fitting. If you get this component right, then cycling will be easier, more enjoyable and faster!

Clothing

In many cases the clothing that you will need for running is not so different from that required for cycling. More specialist equipment can be obtained as you develop. Probably the single most important piece of clothing to enhance comfort, and therefore performance, is a pair of cycling shorts. These are cut specifically to make cycling comfortable and are higher in the back to keep this area warm and covered when learning forward. They have flat seams to prevent rubbing and chafing and a degree of padding in the saddle area. Some shorts are designed specifically for women. Shorts come in a wide variety of sizes, colours and designs.

Generally speaking, the more you pay better quality the shorts will be, but this not mean that an inexpensive pair wil be serviceable and comfortable.

Initially running leggings can be use top of cycling shorts for cooler although they must be close fitting ar the ankle to stop them catching in moving parts of the bicycle. There are p of specially designed cycling leggings o type, made from materials that wil quickly and retain some protection when wet.

When riding on the road the upper must be kept warm and as visible as pos For summer rides something as simp a T-shirt may be enough, although ther many types of cycling jerseys in a ma array of designs.

Gloves are important both for warmtl for protection in case of an accident, cold hands have little control over the b and gears, and hands will almost alwa extended in the case of a crash or fall. G can be either the full-fingered type, w offers protection against the cold, o short-fingered type known as track mit

Although not a legal requiremen riding on the road, the use of a heln common sense. A cycle helmet should the appropriate standards and carry a mark stating that it meets EN1078. will be found on a small label or st inside the helmet. Once you have establ that the helmet is the correct type the fitting must be considered. A he must sit on the head with the strap sn

---

Facing page: An opportunity to train and en the countryside.

underneath the chin to prevent excessive movement, either while riding or in the event of an accident.

Footwear

Footwear can have a significant effect on a triathlete's performance. Cycling shoes allow a much greater transfer of power than trainers and they facilitate a much more accurate position of the foot. Whatever footwear is used, it should be securely fastened and of the correct size. There are a number of different methods of attaching the foot to the pedal. Traditionally, toe clips and ? fitted to the pedals provided a metho securing the foot and aiding the tra of power. Most cyclists now use a cli pedal, of which there are many diff designs. These work on the basic prin that the shoe has some form of plate o bottom that binds to the pedal using a sp system. The pedal releases the foot whe shoe is twisted to the side, but hol securely during normal use. Practice ge into and out of the pedals is necessary will be of particular importance for ti tion training and practice.

Mid-thigh shorts to prevent chafing are characteristic of cycling clothing.

: All competitors must use an appropriate cycle helmet, so training in
nakes perfect sense.

· You will see many types of racing bike in evidence at triathlon events.

Choosing and maintaining your bike

There is a wide range of bicycles available. You may already have a bike in your shed that will do for your first attempt at triathlon, or in the early stages of your training, where any bike can be used. As your aspirations and performance progress, however, you will probably want to move on to what is usually called a racing bike.

Developing a good relationship with a bike shop will prove invaluable. As with all specialist equipment, a good retailer will be able to offer sound advice and provide a range of options based on your considerations.

It is also worth considering the second-hand market. Equipment is often sold from member to member within clubs and this can prove an excellent source of good quality equipment at a reasonable price.

In the space of this book we cannot possibly make you a cycle mechanic, so a relationship with a suitably skilled mechanic or shop will prove valuable. There are, however, a number of checks you ought to run through before starting a session to ensure your bike is safe to ride:

- Saddle and handlebars – check to see if tight
- Brakes – check to see if they work, checking for broken cables or brake-blocks that are not correctly aligned
- Tyres – check that tyre has sufficient pressure and is not worn beyond what would be considered safe
- Saddle height – check it is correct (see bike setup section below)
- Forks – not bent or cracked
- Frames – not damaged or bent
- Wheels – loose/broken spokes or badly buckled
- Handlebars – must have bar end plugs present
- Headset – not too loose or too tight

POSITION AND SET-UP

Correct position on a bicycle is vitally important. Poor matching of individuals to bicycles or bicycles that are not correctly set up can have a major impact on three key areas:

- Safety and control: so you can contro bicycle at all times, especially the bra
- Comfort: to enable you to perform given duration without discomfort
- Efficiency: for optimum power trans any given time

It is important that, in order to achieve criteria, the bike must be made to fi cyclist and not the cyclist to fit the bik

Three key areas should be examined considering a rider's optimum position bike: foot position; saddle height pos and tilt; and stem height and extensior handlebar width and position.

Since the human body comes in a s ingly infinite number of shapes and any formulae can be used only as sta points. Despite the guidelines and cal tions presented here, it is also importa consider how the cyclist actually feels o bike. Even though many experienced cy and triathletes have used trial and error establishing a regular riding position, few using this method can neverthele entirely sure that they have achievec optimum position.

Foot position

Because this aspect of position has an ence on many other areas of set-up, w look at this first. Incorrect foot positic can lead very quickly to injury. It is a fundamental area of power transfei therefore it is vital to achieve the cc position. The centre of the ball of the should be directly over the centre o pedal spindle and the foot should n ally be parallel with the cranks. This i optimum position for high power o and a high cadence. There may be occ to allow variations to this. Some cy for example, may find a 'heels in' or out' position to be more natural. T acceptable so long as this is establ as being a natural tendency. To check rider's natural foot position, ask him c to sit on a table with legs dangling.

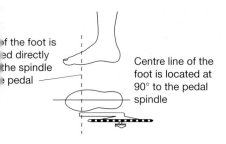

of the foot is
ed directly
the spindle
e pedal

Centre line of the foot is located at 90° to the pedal spindle

orrect way to set up the foot position on
edals.

le height position and tilt

is probably the single most important
urement with regards to bike fit. This
e has, in the past, been tied very closely
frame size. With the increasing popu-
of compact design frames, and the pos-
y that you will have a bike other than
ard road bikes, this measurement is no
r as useful.

order to arrive at an optimum saddle
t we first need to measure the rider's
n (inside leg). The saddle height can
be calculated by multiplying the inseam
factor of 0.885, for example:

eam of 83cm × 0.885 = 73.5

addle height will therefore be 73.5cm
e centre of the bottom bracket. When
gure is applied to the bike, the rider's

leg should not be locked out. There should
be a slight bend at the knee when the pedal
is in line with the seat tube.

Numerous other formulae can be applied
to calculate the saddle height. Multiplying
the rider's inseam by a factor of 1.09, for
example, gives a height that also includes the
crank arm. This calculation can be varied
slightly to allow for anatomical differences,
particularly between male and female riders.
The degree of variance should not exceed
0.03. Therefore the lowest calculation you
should complete is inseam × 1.06, and the
highest calculation that should be completed
is inseam × 1.12.

The simplest method to determine saddle
height is for the rider to sit on their bike
with their heels on the pedals. Set the pedal
to its lowest position (in line with the seat
tube) and the leg should be straight, without
overstretching. It is important to note that
there should be no rocking of the hips from
side to side. This position may, however, be
too low for many cyclists, so you may have
to raise the saddle by 1–2cm to achieve the
most comfortable position.

Once you have arrived at your optimum
measurement this needs to be applied to the
bike. The measurement you have relates to
the distance between the top of the saddle
and the centre of the pedal axle. Slight alter-
ation may need to be made for the pedal
and shoe combination and type being
used. Additional factors that may affect this

this measurement you can
w far forward the knee
come when the pedal is at
ck. This will dictate how far
he saddle is positioned.

urement are: clothing thickness and
 leg length discrepancies; flexibility;
le type and design including suspen-
where fitted, and pedalling style.

nce the correct saddle height has been
ved, the position and tilt of the saddle
need to be considered. Saddle position
:asured relative to the bottom bracket
k axle) and the rails of the saddle
 fore and aft movement. The angle of
:at tube of the bike frame will play an
rtant role in this adjustment and you
ïnd seat tube angles varying between
d 75 degrees. A reliable measurement
take a plumb line and see if the cyclist's
sits over the pedal axle when the cranks
orizontal.

**height, extension, handlebar
h and position**

idea behind this assumes that this
on allows the best power transfer. This
urement again has its limitations, since
ïngle of the foot varies throughout
»edal revolution depending on indi-
l technique. Many successful cyclists
triathletes have used knee positions
it forward of this point. For this reason
 a variance of 2cm from the plumb

ddles should be set parallel to the
ïd or with a very slight upward tilt at
ose. This will vary slightly depending
ïe shape of the saddle used. If the nose
e saddle tilts down too much, weight
e pushed onto the arms, causing undue
ïe and discomfort. Many women tilt the
e down in an attempt to reduce the
ure on the groin. In this instance, it
d be advisable to seek a more suitable
e. A saddle tilting up generally indicates
he saddle height is too low; conversely
dle tilting down indicates one that is a
too high. Check the saddle height (*see*
65) and readjust as necessary.

3 page: A well set-up bike will enhance
rt and efficiency.

Reach is defined as the distance between
the centre of the saddle and the centre of
the handlebars. Influencing factors on this
measurement are the length of the cyclist's
arm and back, the degree of flexibility and
the size of their hands, and the position they
are trying to achieve. Once pedal position
and saddle height, position and tilt have been
established, the only factors that have influ-
ence over the reach are frame size (non-
adjustable), stem length and handlebar
selection.

When using drop bars, although cyclists
may spend more time holding the tops of
the bars or the brake hoods, they should be
able to reach the drops quite comfortably.

The bottom section of the bars should be
parallel with the floor or slightly tilted
upwards. When on the drops, the cyclist
should have a slight bend at the elbow to
allow some suspension when riding rather
than having the arms locked rigid. The elbow
should just clear the knee (a gap of 1–4cm)
when the crank is at its most forward position. This should leave the back nearly horizontal without causing the cyclist to come
forward on the saddle.

Women may need less reach because of
their relatively shorter torso and arms, and
because of this they will also have less difference between saddle and handlebar height.
As women generally have a greater degree
of flexibility, however, they may be able to
tolerate a greater difference. While this may
prove aerodynamic, it will probably lead to a
loss of power and leverage.

The use of tri-bars and/or low-profile bars
is also commonplace in triathlon. These are
designed to lower the frontal area that you
present to the wind. By doing this you can
become more aerodynamic and subsequently
faster. Many triathletes, however, adjust the
position to such an extent that it has a detrimental effect on the critical measurements
surrounding the position of the body in relation to the pedals. This sacrifices efficiency
and the transfer of power is reduced. To
prevent this you must be very careful when
setting up any such bars. You should be
looking for a position that maintains the position of the hips and legs in relation to the

pedals and bottom bracket, while allowing you to lower the position of the head and shoulders and bring the arms closer together. This may take some trial and error but, providing you are moving at speeds in excess of around 25km/h, the effects will be advantageous. Riding in this position obviously compromises the amount of control you can exert on the bike, and should only be undertaken on straight roads where you have good visibility and are aware of potential risks. Practise, at first on a static trainer or on quiet roads, will help you become accustomed to the position.

Many triathletes and cyclists use static training equipment within their training programmes, allowing some cycling activity to be undertaken without venturing outside. This is of particular use at night or in weather conditions that are not favourable to cycling. Sessions can also be undertaken on the trainers, often referred to as turbo trainers, that cannot be replicated safely on the road. For example, some particularly hard sprints or sustained efforts can be difficult or unsafe on the road owing to obstacles and the need to concentrate on traffic. Turbo trainers normally fix the back wheel of a bike within an A-frame and then hold it against a rolling surface. This in turn is attached to some method of creating resistance. In older models this is literally a fan that creates air resistance and provides something to work against. Some models have a magnetic or oil-based resistance system. These are generally quieter than the fan-based systems but more expensive. Price is usually an indicator of quality.

CYCLING TECHNIQUE

Many people assume that there is little technique involved in cycling. This can be a convenient perception given the difficult techniques that must be learnt and practised in swimming. Compared with the intricacies of swimming, cycling can indeed look simple, but there are still a number of techniques that must be practised and mastered to make a successful athlete:

- Mounting (stationary and on the mo
- Dismounting (stationary and on the m
- Pedalling
- Gear selection and changing
- Cornering
- Climbing and descending
- Group riding

Mounting and dismounting

It may sound obvious, but there are basic points to remember when mount stationary bike:

- Place both hands on handlebars
- Apply front brake
- Mount the bike from the left-side
- Swing leg over saddle and put onto floor
- Adjust the position of the right-hand to about 2 o'clock
- Put right foot onto pedal ready to down
- Check over right shoulder
- Push with right foot and move bo onto saddle
- Adjust position and accelerate

Dismounting is the same action in rev This will ensure you can start and end safely.

Many experienced triathletes have tered a faster transition by being ab mount and dismount the bike without h to be entirely stationary. This skill is useful and will give the athlete a much movement from running to cycling visa versa. There are a number of met of mounting and dismounting on the and the adaptation of these methods to you will depend on the use of clipless ling pedals or running shoes for cyclir you are using running or training shoe cycling you have a simpler job, althoug we have discussed, you will have to acc loss of power transfer. If you are using cy

Facing page: Setting up and using tri-bars w take some practice.

shoes and clipless pedals you need to decide if you will be attaching the shoes to the bike before you mount or putting on your shoes and attempting to run. Running in cycling shoes is not easy, nor is it often safe. Cycling shoes have little grip on the bottoms and are not designed for running. The fastest triathletes through a transition zone will usually have their shoes ready attached to the pedals. They run barefoot from the swim to the point where you can mount the bike and then put their feet into the pedals once moving. This is an advanced skill, but once mastered it will save you many seconds in transition.

When practising mounting on the move, find a quiet area for your first attempts, if possible, and use a forgiving surface such as grass. Run with both hands on the top of the handlebars. You now have two options. The first is simply to jump from the back of the bike so that your bottom lands on the saddle; you can then position the feet on

the pedals and accelerate away, if nece putting your feet into shoes that you attached to the pedals. The second me also starts with both hands on the har bars. While running slightly more slo place the outside foot (the one furthest from the bike, depending on which side prefer) onto the pedal and use the insid to scoot along, providing some speed you can bring the inside leg around the of the saddle onto the pedal and adjust bottom onto the seat. The second me is much less painful, although it does re some practice, and is also much easier t in reverse.

If using cycling shoes you need to tise putting them on when attached to pedals and while riding along. Elastic b can be used to hold them in a flat pos by placing the cranks at 3 o'clock 9 o'clock; this can give you a flat surfac which to place the foot. Once you have s cient momentum you can then briefly p

Triathlon cycling courses are very varied.

eting in a non-drafting race, but still with other
around. Be aware of the rules.

ling and put the foot into the pedal.
explanation probably does not do justice
e intricacies of this technique. Watching
sed elite triathlons will give you a much
r idea of how to apply the technique
ur transitions.

lling

this seems very simple, but if you
get this right you will be much more
ent and therefore a much faster tri-
e. The novice triathlete should practise
ling at a brisk cadence. Cadence is the
at which you move the pedals around
s measured in revolutions per minute
), one revolution being one entire circle
one foot. The ideal rpm is between 80
00 revolutions per minute. When you
start this will feel very quick and you
feel that the gears you are using to
ve this rpm are too low. Persist with
nd you will become much more effi-
. Put simply, if you can only ever pedal
y you will struggle to go truly fast, since
re relying on pushing the pedals hard.

If you can pedal fast, however, and have the
ability to push the pedals hard when necessary, you will be much, much faster.

Gear selection and changing

By following the above guidelines you will
find that gear selection is in many ways
already made for you, since you will need to
change gear if you find your cadence drop-
ping. The key to maintaining momentum is
to change gear before you need to and to
ease the pressure off the pedals as you change
gear. This will ensure you get a smooth
change and do not lose any momentum.

Cornering

Many good cyclists have made mistakes
when cornering that have cost them a great
deal of pain and skin. Our objective when
cornering is to get around the corner as
quickly and as smoothly as possible. To do
this we must make certain preparations
before we start to turn:

- Assess the surface for potential slippage problems
- Make sure you are in the gear you need to exit the corner
- Brake before you need to start turning using the rear brake gently
- Move your weight onto the leg on the outside of the direction you will be turning
- Look to the point at which you will be exiting the corner
- Do not pedal through the corner
- Draw a line which is as straight as possible through the corner and follow this as closely as is safe to do so
- Accelerate out of the corner

Again, practising cornering will ensure you are confident and able to handle different corners in different circumstances. Be very careful in the wet and in icy conditions. Practise on corners you are familiar with and then transfer this skill as you cycle in new areas.

Climbing and descending

You will inevitably come across a triathlon course that takes in hills. Practising going up and coming down will help keep you safe as well as making you a faster athlete. Climbing is a combination of pacing yourself and using the skills we have discussed above regarding pedalling and gear selection. Many cyclists climb out of the saddle, which is a skill in itself. The best way of practising this is on a turbo trainer where you can be safe. Use a gear that is a little higher than you need to maintain cadence and then push down with one leg, using the resistance to raise the body up off the saddle. You need to maintain the body weight over or just slightly forward of the saddle and use the arms to support you in this position as well as the resistance of the pedals to hold the body up. Being out of the saddle allows you to use your body weight to push the pedals down, although overall it is harder work because you are using more of the body in the pedalling action. A combination of pedalling in and out of the saddle is best to prevent fatigue but to maintain pace.

When descending, the cornering skil[l] have discussed are applied at speed. The way of staying safe and fast is to look a ahead as possible and predict, rather react to, the conditions that are present

Group riding

While for most people triathlon is a s non-drafting event, there are occasions the ability to ride in a group is useful. Cy can take up many hours and comple hours out on the road in a group ca much more enjoyable. Group session also a good way of injecting some speed your training. In order to do this sa however, you must master some basic in group riding. Communication is the to safe riding, so let others around you k what you are doing and, if you are at front, what you can see. Experienced g riders ride very close to one another, t especially common in cycling clubs. Do be afraid of this and make sure you smooth and predictable. Do not ride your hands on the brakes and try to fo the wheel in front as closely as possible. kind of riding takes some practice, but mastered can be very enjoyable.

With some basic skills mastered we move on to looking at how we are goin train on the bike. Skills training can b integral part of your cycling preparation can be done on an easy or rest day, viding you are only practising skills.

TRAINING FOR CYCLING

This section deals with how to appl cycling the principles of developing fi already discussed in Chapter 2. Athletes have experience of cycling clubs wil doubt have been made aware of the typ training available to them. The mai of most cycling clubs is the traditional n ing club run. This type of training is dominantly of long, steady duration, w develops aerobic fitness. While training group is not the only way of develo this kind of fitness, group training will

...ng is a combination of skill, practice and physical training.
... required to be a successful triathlete.

...re tolerable as the duration involved
...2 hours and above for medium-
...nce racing, or more than 3½ hours for
...er distances) can be tedious for all
...the most disciplined of individuals.
...p riding can be daunting and care
...ld be taken when starting out in this
...ne aspect of cycling skill. Nevertheless
...an be a great way of developing group
...g skills.

...val training: DIRT principles

...e intense training will be needed to
...op the other areas of fitness that impact
...ycling performance. Interval training
...d play an important part in the devel-
...nt of cycling performance. By using the
...iples given above, you can develop your
...ffective and enjoyable interval training
...ns.

When constructing cycling training sets, the following variables should be used and controlled:

$D =$ Distance, e.g. 100m, 1km etc.

$I =$ Interval of rest – using either time as a control of the set or a control of the rest. Within cycling this is easy, because the bike allows you to keep rolling with very little effort to recover or to pedal gently to aid recovery

$R =$ How many repetitions, e.g. 20, 30, 40

$T =$ Time – a target for each repetition. This can be time to cover a certain distance or as a control, as detailed above

Designing a cycling training programme by DIRT principles			
	January	*March*	*May*
$D =$	2 minutes as hard as possible	4 minutes hard effort	5 minutes hard effort
$I =$	with 30 secs rest	with 90 secs rest	with 90 secs res
$R =$	× 9	× 12	× 15
$T =$	Hold 90 rpm* pedalling speed	Hold 90 rpm pedalling speed	Hold 90 rpm pedalling speed

* revolutions per minute

Riding out of the saddle can produce additional power, but at some physical cost.

g alone and racing alone.

ntrolling these variables, training ses-
can be produced that give control of
ne, duration, intensity, rest and speed
hapter 2). The sets are measurable and
e logged. The above set construction
itself to the application of training over-
nd progression.

PING YOUR BALANCE

thing already said in Chapter 2 regard-
he creation of a balanced swimming
ng programme applies equally well to
g. Top competitive cyclists can train
nything up to thirty hours per week.
riathlete, however, must balance cycling
ng with two other disciplines, and many
s will decide this balance. With careful
ing, however, sessions can be inte-
d.

cycle training

use of static trainers or turbo trainers
cle training has been common practice

for a number of years now. These trainers
have a number of benefits:

- Constant conditions
- Safe
- Traffic-free
- Focus on physical conditioning, not bike-
  handling skills
- Cyclists of different abilities can train
  together

However, there are also downsides to this
type of training:

- Boredom
- Lack of technique training
- Riders become less traffic conscious
- Does not develop confidence in ability
- Potential for individuals to get too hot
- Novices may not have the right equip-
  ment

These types of trainers can allow you to run
fitness-specific training sessions and work on
technique in ways that may not be possible
on the road.

Cycling's many disciplines

There are many cycling disciplines and a brief understanding of the structure of cycling may suggest the variety of potential training sessions.

Track cycling
Carried out on hard-banked tracks, either outdoors or indoors, and sometimes on grass tracks, this kind of cycling uses a bike with a fixed gear and no brakes. There are many types of races lasting from as little as 500m through to 20km. This kind of riding develops a rider's cadence and ability to achieve and sustain high speeds for a relatively short space of time.

BMX/Cycle speedway
Very short duration races on specific bikes. Excellent for developing very short-term power.

Off-road cycling
This can take the form of mountain biking or cyclo-cross. Both of these forms of riding develop aerobic ability, lactate threshold and, most importantly, bike-handling ability.

Road racing
Group riding on a standard road bike. Distances for novices can vary between 25 and 100km. The constantly changing pace develops a rider's aerobic ability, lactate threshold and short-term power. Bike-handling also benefits.

Time trials
Solo riding (though sometimes in small groups) on a standard road bike or specific

time-trial or triathlon machine. Compl the course in the shortest possible Distances vary from 16 to 160km (10 miles). Excellent training for non-dra triathletes.

DESIGNING YOUR CYCLING TRAINING PROGRAMME

So far we have looked at the equip requirements for cycling and at some o sessions you may use to develop the n sary skills. Now you understand what cycling training programme will involve time to build up your endurance acco to the 10 per cent rule (*see* Chapter 1 develop the specific components of fi required. Plan the targets and conte your training sessions by looking at the planner you completed and highlight you will be going cycling. Take the data your basic endurance and speed tests ar yourself goals and objectives for the sess

The volume of cycling that you will to do will depend very much on your t event. If you are completing an Iro event you will need much more endur; based training than an athlete preparin a sprint or even a standard distance e You have already established some basic for your cycling and you know how fa can cycle and how long this takes. App the 10 per cent rule will give you a starting point for planning your cycle tra for endurance. There are a number of aspects you may also like to consider. I are targeting a specific time, for exan then speed will be a major factor. Wor the average speed you will need to ma

Calculation of average speed		
Distance	*Time taken*	*Average speed*
20km	55 minutes	20 ÷ 55 × 60 = 21.8km/h
40km	1 hour 20 minutes	40 ÷ 80 × 60 = 30km/h
180km	5.5 hours	180 ÷ 330 × 60 = 32.7km/h

hieve the split in cycling that will give
our overall time. This will depend on
strengths in the other disciplines but
d not be too hard to calculate. Once
have this target average you need to
lish how far away you are from main-
g this speed over the distance required.
involves a test over the distance, fol-
d by some simple of maths to establish
average speed.
u now need to increase your average
d in training. Accelerate to just above
target speed and hold it for a short
Start with 2 minutes and then increase
y stages of a minute until you can hold
inutes at your desired pace. You need
ow between 1 and 3 minutes of easy
between intervals to recover. The fol-
g three examples may supply some
nce:

minutes warm up (steadily increase the
nsity over this time until you feel
rm and ready to start)
minutes at 22km/h
inutes very easy
mplete the sequence (2 minutes on, 3
nutes off) five times
minutes cool down (steadily decrease
e effort with some light, yet brisk,
dalling throughout)

must maintain the cadence targets dis-
d above in the pedalling section.

minutes warm up
inutes at 22km/h
inutes very easy
mplete the sequence (4 minutes on,
minutes off) seven times
rm down

minutes warm up
inutes at 22km/h
inute very easy

Interval training will produce a race-ready athlete
if planned well.

– Complete the sequence (6 minutes on,
  1 minute off) ten times
– Warm down

If there is a large gap between your current
speed ability and your target speed, you can
repeat this process of overloading and developing speed in a number of stages. You
could, for example, complete the above sets
over a number of weeks to build up to an
average speed of 22km/h. Then start again,
going back to set one but setting a target
rate of 26km/h. By going through this
process at increasing speeds over the weeks
and months, you can build the ability to ride
faster. You will also be developing your
endurance by simply riding longer, which
incidentally will contribute to your strength
and speed as well.

Rules of triathlon: cycling

An understanding of the competition rules that apply to each discipline in triathlon is essen
The following rules are as detailed by the British Triathlon Association, although they bro
apply also to International Triathlon Union races and Ironman races.

11.1 Bicycles must be well maintained, roadworthy and have the following characteristics:

    a. No more than two (2) metres long and 75 centimetres wide

    b. Measure at least 24 centimetres from the ground to the centre of the chain w
axle

    c. A vertical line touching the front-most point of the saddle will be no more tha
centimetres in front of and no more than 15 centimetres behind a vertical line pas
through the centre of the chain wheel axle. A competitor must not have the capab
of adjusting the saddle beyond these limits during competition

    d. Measure no less than 54 centimetres and no more than 65 centimetres betwee
vertical line passing through the centre of the chain wheel axle and a vertical
through the centre of the front wheel axle. Exceptions may be given for the bicy
of children and very tall or very short competitors

    e. Windbreaks or other bodywork or other substantial means of reducing wind resist
on machines is prohibited

    f. The front wheel may be a different diameter than the rear wheel but must be of sp
construction. Wheel covers or disc wheels are allowed on the rear wheel only

    g. No wheel may contain mechanisms that are capable of accelerating it

    h. There must be a brake on each wheel

    i. Handlebars must be plugged

    j. Add-ons such as computer or lighting brackets and mounting points must be positic
so as to prevent injury in the event of a crash or collision with other competitor
spectators. NOTE: this also applies to mountain bike handlebar extensions

11.2 Cycles must be marked with the competitor's number, a suitable label should be provi
by the organizer

11.3 Approved cycling safety helmets of ANSI Z90.4, SNELL B90, EN 1078 or an equiva
national standard must be worn by competitors. (NOTE: a CE mark is NOT an appr
mark.)

11.4 Helmets must remain structurally unaltered, elastic chin straps are not permitted

11.5 Helmets and cycles will be checked to ensure that they meet the above requirements
race official. This does not certify that bikes are roadworthy or helmets are safe. It is
responsibility of every competitor to ensure that their helmet and cycle meet the requ
ments. Competitors who fail to do so may, for reasons of safety, be prevented f
participating

unning

he final discipline in the triathlon,
ing presents a specific challenge. You
be fatigued after the previous swim and
but you still have a race to finish.

JIPMENT

the equipment requirements for
ng, the kit you will need for running
ook very simple. Your concern will be
d to ensuring that it is safe and effec-
To assist with this there are some basic
lines:

ning

the clothing going to keep you warm
ough and/or will it ensure that you do
t become overheated?
the clothing suitable for the weather
nditions, waterproof, etc.?
ll the clothing hinder the activity? Is it
tight or too baggy?
ll the clothing pose any safety prob-
ns? Baggy clothing can cause you to
p and fall

wear

the footwear designed for the purpose?
all-purpose training shoe will be suffi-
nt in most cases, although a specific
nning trainer is preferred
the footwear correctly fitted? Many
ople do not lace or tie up shoes cor-
tly
he footwear in a serviceable condition?
ry worn training shoes with holes and
er damage may prove dangerous

• Is the footwear suitable for the weather?
A very light racing spike may not be suitable for a winter track session

A specialist running shop is the best place to
source appropriate running shoes. It may be
able to offer a podiatry test and sell you running shoes that specifically meet your needs.
It will also stock running-specific clothing that
you may not find in large non-specific sports
stores. Running leggings tend to be close-
fitting with foot loops. Base layers, which
help move sweat away from the body, can also
be used and a good-quality running jacket
will also prove useful. Much of the running
clothing can be used when cycling to help
keep down cost and volume of kit.

Many aspiring triathletes come into the
sport from a running background. The run
segment is probably the least technical
of the three disciplines, but the sensation of
putting one foot in front of the other is very
different when preceded by a bike section of
20 to 180km, and only remotely resembles
the normally smooth-flowing action of
single-sport running. This unusual sensation
is brought about by the circular action of
cycling. Although the legs do most of the
work in both the bike and run sections, the
individual muscles in the upper and lower
leg are contracting in a different way when
running.

Because the running section has been preceded by swim and cycle sections, there is
an increased likelihood that fatigue can be a
limiting factor in performance. The ability
to overcome this fatigue and to run fast and
efficiently at the same time can be a major
factor in successfully completing an event in
an acceptable time.

Running is perhaps the least technical of the disciplines, but no less demanding.

There are no shortcuts to becoming a good triathlon runner. Technique, speed, strength and mobility training, together with an awareness of the specific requirements of triathlon running, will lead to longer and faster performances.

TECHNIQUE

Runners have differing techniques, some of which are more efficient than others. Running styles are governed, to a certain extent, by limb length, body shape and fitness levels. Although there is a limit to how much a running style can be changed, improvements are always possible. The basic principle of endurance running is:

Speed = Stride length × Stride frequency

The leg action necessary for good running technique can be divided into four phases.

Front support phase

The objective of this phase is to mini deceleration at foot strike. With each the foot contacts the ground on the of the foot that is most natural for athlete. For most athletes the outsic the heel strikes first in longer, slower and the mid of the forefoot contacts in shorter, faster races. The suppor cushions the ground contact in a contr way to minimize braking forces. Arm a is similar to sprinting, but less active or nounced.

Drive phase

The objective of this phase is to opti the forward drive. The athlete's weight over the foot and off the toe of the : Hips, knees and ankle joints extend d this phase; in longer distance races, how this extension may not be complete.

Guidelines for a good running technique

...d	Should be still with little up and down movement, looking forward
...s	Bent at the elbow to approximately 90 degrees, relaxed, movement should be forward as well as across the body, and movements should be small, controlled and efficient
...nk	Erect, relaxed, hips forward
...lders	Relaxed, loose
...strike	Under body, either in mid-sole, side of foot or heel. Foot should be pointing forward
...e off	Push off quickly after foot strike, heel should come up towards the buttocks
...de length	Comfortable and in proportion to body
...ence	Optimum is around 180 strides per minute (90 strikes per foot per minute)

...kit should be comfortable for every ...ine.

As the final discipline, the run can seem like the longest for many novice triathletes.

In analysing your action it would help to consult a coach, who should observe the action of the athlete's feet from the rear, side and front, the extension of the hips, knees and ankles, and check for the efficiency of the action.

Recovery phase

The objective of this phase is to contribute to an efficient action and rhythm. This phase begins with the foot breaking contact with the ground, with the trailing leg flexing at the knee and then moving up towards the backside. The height that the heel is brought towards the backside, and the degree of flexion at the knee, is dependent on running speed. This is more pronounced in sprinting activities and less pronounced at slower running speeds.

Forward swinging phase

The objective of this phase of the leg cycle is to prepare for an active foot strike. The recovery leg swings through past the body and upward, but this is less pronounced than in sprinting. Generally, the slower the speed, the lower the knee lift. Once the leg has passed to the front of the body, with the hip flexed, the leg will lower and the knee will extend. The foot then moves down and back relative to the body in preparation to minimize braking at foot strike.

As a general guideline, the body should always be over the lead foot as it strikes the ground. If this is not the case the stride length is too long: the foot striking ahead of the body will apply a braking force before the body passes over the foot, thus slowing the athlete down. Ideally the foot plant should be in a straight line to the direction of travel, so ensuring that the forces at the take-off phase are propelling the athlete forward. Do not worry if you are displaying other characteristics such as splay footing or pigeon toeing, unless this is a clear problem or it is creating injury issues. If you suspect that this is the case, you should seek out the attention of a physiotherapist to correct the fault.

TRAINING FOR RUNNING

Drills, widely referred to in both run swim coaching sessions, are designe develop running action. They are si specific practices used to emphasize improve a component of technique. act by isolating and concentrating on one aspect of the running action. Man athlons are won and lost on the run sec of the course, not through lack of sta but through an inability to perform ar cient running style. Some basic running given here should help improve your run efficiency.

The various drills are not fixed, ar spending time working with coaches will develop additional drills that ca applied to your sessions. When desig a drill you need to consider what aspe technique it is designed to improve, as as the technique of actually conductin drill itself.

When using drills to improve tech you should ensure that you are not fat beforehand. Drills should therefor included after the warm up at the sta the session, when the main aim is to im technique. Drills should be carried out a short distance (25–50m) with a back to facilitate recovery. They shou repeated between three and six times. the main component is introduced afte drills, you should keep in mind the pu of the drills and focus on this durin next component of the session.

Drills can also be very beneficial in a as a recovery session. This is because move the limbs through a greater ran motion, helping in the recovery proce maintaining the range of movement dynamic flexibility. When used in the w up phase, take care to ensure that yo fully warm before doing the drill, since extend the limbs outside the normal of motion.

Facing page: A demonstration of the phases group of elite athletes.

	Basic running drills	
Drill	*Technique*	*Purpose*
High knees	Short, very fast steps lifting knees high in front of the body	• Improves running cadence • Improves recovery phase of trail leg • Improves range of motion fr[o] the hip
Kick backs	With hands on bottom, kick feet back to touch the hands using a fast action	• Improves running cadence • Improves recovery of trail leg • Improves stride length
Arm drives	As high knees, but focus on driving arms through and pumping	• Improves upper body alignm[e] • Improves coordination and a[n] balance
Hills	15–30 seconds uphill running on a steepish slope	• Improves stride length • Improves push off
Striding a) b)	Focus on arm action, all movement Arm drive Head position	• Reduces excess movement driving forward. Focus on keeping head still
Downhill running	Lean slightly forward, 'float', avoid braking	• Improves leg cadence • Improves stride length
Long rear legs	Make singular effort to push ground away. Leave foot in contact with ground a fraction longer than normal	• Improves the recovery phase of the cycle

Distance training

The overall aim is to complete the race distance at a comfortable pace, subsequently building confidence. Distance training also serves to increase running efficiency and aerobic endurance. When first planning these sessions the terrain should be flat and unchallenging, since the distance covered will represent the main challenge. It is also important that, owing to the prolonged nature of these types of sessions, the actual running surface should be closely considered.

Running on grass, off-road or on tartan running tracks is much better than on asphalt roads and pavements, as these will greatly reduce the impact to the lower limbs. A[s] improve in fitness, ability and confid[ence] the use of hilly courses can add to the i[nten]sity of the session. Novices may initiall[y] that it is more useful to work on time [more] than distance.

The distances covered in triathlon [train]ing can be up to twice the race dis[tance] for sprint and standard-distance even[ts] up to race distance for long-distance e[vents] This type of training should be empha[sised] during the first half of the training [pro]gramme if you are planning on incre[asing] your pace, or it can be the entire foc[us of] the programme if your target is just to [com]plete the event.

h swimming, drills will enhance your
que and ultimately your performance.

val training

...se of interval training has been dis-
...d in both the swimming and running
...les. Its application within running is
...similar. The purpose of this section
...assist you in identifying the ways in
...intervals can be applied to running.
...al training is governed by:

...tance
...ensity
...etition
...ie

For a novice athlete an introductory interval
session may be:

Run 1 minute, walk 1 minute, ten times

In this example both the distance and the
density are governed by a fixed-time work
interval, repeated ten times.

As an athlete progresses so should the
intervals. A further example for a more
advanced athlete is:

Run as hard as possible for 200m of a
track, jog 200m for recovery, ten times

Here the distance is governed by the 200m
of the track. The intensity is governed by
'as hard as possible', although it could quite
easily be determined by a target time for
each 200m work interval. The repetition is
defined as twelve, though again if you are
using a target time for the 200m work
interval you could increase the repetitions
until you are unable to make the target time.
Time is a factor here only if a target time is
applied.

As you make further progress you can
introduce some changes:

• Reduce the rest periods
• Increase the intensity of the work periods
  (running faster/harder)
• Increase the distance/length of the rest
  periods

Do not, however, try to change all three
variables at once, as this could possibly lead
to injury and overtraining.

Strength training

Strength training in running is a conten-
tious subject. It is widely accepted that
an increase in specific muscle strength can
improve running efficiency by increasing the strength of individual and specific
muscles, so that fewer fibres are recruited
for a given workload. If a runner, for example, develops stronger running muscles,
these muscles would be more efficient at

ing shoulder to shoulder gives a real competitive experience.

elling them while running. This would
to a reduction in the number of fibres
ited to propel him at a given speed.
is also widely acknowledged that core
ity training (the training of the muscles
stabilize the trunk of the body) is ben-
l to increasing a runner's efficiency
igh eliminating excessive movement
the trunk, thus transferring the
num power through the body and onto
oad.
e development of overall body strength
de these two specific areas, however, is
ely to produce any significant benefits
nning and may cause hypertrophy within
les, leading to an increase in muscle
mass (bulk) in muscles not specifically related
to running that will have a detrimental effect
on efficiency.

When looking to develop additional
running-specific strength, the use of various
running training methods needs to be
considered before non-running training is
deployed. Hill running, resistance running
and aqua jogging can all play a part in this.
If you feel that you might benefit from
specific non-running strength training, you
are advised to contact a suitably qualified
instructor (NVQ level 2 or above, Coaching,
Teaching & Instruction) to assist you in
delivering this. The same situation applies to
the development of core stability.

g page: Intervals create the stress of racing in a controlled training environment.

Rules of triathlon: running

There are few rules relating specifically to the run section in triathlon, although many people get penalized for infringements of the race number rules. The following rules are as detailed the British Triathlon Association, although they broadly apply also to International Triath Union races and Ironman races.

12.1 Race organizers must provide numbers made of suitable material. The BTA appro numbers printed on Tyvek® and these are a mandatory requirement for organizers National Championship and Grand Prix National Ranking Series Events. Other Stand distance events (1,500m swim, 40km bike and 10km run) and above are recommended use Tyvek to minimize the risk of problems caused by torn or lost race numbers

12.2 The maximum size of race number should be 225mm × 225mm

12.3 See section 16 for competition rules relating to race numbers

Race technique training

As part of your preparations you need to include some of the techniques that will be employed during a typical race. Sessions need to include:

- Accelerating out of corners
- Mixed pace running
- Responding to forced acceleration
- Choosing the best line
- Drafting
- Dead turns
- Downhill running
- Uphill running

ansition

lon is unique in its structure as the tion element of the event requires an of technical expertise that is unlikely to been learnt from other sports. For es to triathlon, the transition generally ces more queries than any other area sport.

need to break the transition into its onent parts:

nsition 1 (T1): the transition from the im to the cycle
nsition 2 (T2): the transition from the le to the run

onsiderations and guidelines for these tions are different, although the main tive in both is to exit transition as y as possible.

e key to good transition is planning preparation. By organizing the right ment in the right place transition can de a much smoother process.

nsition practice will allow you to familyourself with the procedures of transio that you will not be caught out on lay.

athlon makes great demands on the vascular, muscular and central nervous ns. Each discipline uses different coms of muscles, intensities of loadspeeds of contraction and rhythm. major muscles needed in the swim are the upper body. The water supports weight, but upon exiting the water the body transfers from the horizontal position to the vertical and the blood supply demands a rapid change from the upper body to the lower body; this can create a feeling of dizziness or disorientation, particularly in novice athletes. The main muscles used in cycling are in the lower and middle body. The bike supports the weight, but in the transition from bike to run the type of contraction in the quadriceps, in particular, changes from concentric and non-weight bearing with aided recovery to concentric and eccentric contraction. In the run itself the lower body again does most of the work; the main difference lies in the type of contraction and the fact that two to three times the body weight is taken on each contact with the ground.

There is no set method for transition, although there are a number of skills and shortcuts that can produce an effective transition technique when combined:

- Swim. Race number worn underneath wetsuit either on race belt or pinned to vest (or trisuit)
- Swim (pool or warm-weather open water). Specific triathlon clothing can be worn during the swim, bike and run sections without modification
- Bike. Cycling shoes ready clipped into the bike pedals
- Bike. Mount the bike on the move from the mounting line rather than mounting from a stationary position

NSITION 1

letes leave the water and run into the
tion area, which can sometimes be at
100m away. If the event has included
en water swim, you should be removing
wetsuit while on the move, preparing
roll the vest and/or the number belt
underneath it. The effort of these com-
 actions puts a great physical strain on
ody, as oxygen demand is high: it has
apt to a full weight-bearing activity
 moving very fast and performing
lex motor skills. By the time you enter
ansition area you should be almost free
 wetsuit and the number should either
 place or ready to be put into place as
as possible.
on arriving at the bike, and before even
ing it, put on your helmet and sun-
s, if applicable (these are usually placed
 the helmet). Then take the bike out
 rack before proceeding towards the
tion exit. Upon reaching the mounting
'scoot' the bike along and then mount
the move, before putting your feet into
oes already attached to the pedals.

NSITION 2

bike-to-run transition should be very
 as you can loosen your shoes before
ng at the dismounting line. Dismount
e move and then proceed towards
acking point. Rack your bike before
ving the helmet and then put on
ng shoes (preferably with lace lock
n/elastic laces in place for speed) and
proceed towards the T2 exit to embark
 the run.

The adjustment between cycling and
running is often very difficult, but this element of transition can be made much easier
through practice. One problem faced by
novice and experienced triathletes alike is
the issue of identifying their station. Care
should be taken when setting up to help you
find your transition station in the heat of
competition. Since preparation is the key to
a successful transition, always follow detailed
checklists:

Pre-race

• Check race gear
• Ensure running shoes have elastic laces
  and lace locks in place
• Secure number to vest or race belt

Race day

• Arrive early
• Find racking stations and walk through
  transition, identifying entry and exit points
  for T1 and T2
• Check the location of the mount/
  dismount line
• Prepare footwear (talc or Vaseline as
  preferred/required)
• Ensure bike is in correct gear to start off
• Use Vaseline on cuffs/ankle/collar of
  wetsuit to aid removal and prevent
  chaffing
• Ensure feeding bottles are prepared
• Rack bike
• Lay out equipment in logical order
• Get changed and go race!

page: The exit from the water is the start
 transition period, a physical and mental
nge.

Transition rules and regulations

should be aware of the British Triathlon rules as they apply to competition. Pay particular ntion to the following excerpts during transition training and general competition.

General rules

TE: in the case of a child taking part in an event it is the responsibility of the Parent(s) and/or mpanying Adult(s) to ensure that the child understands these rules and that the child's pment, clothing, etc., is suitable, maintained, correctly prepared and used. See also the itional Rules for Children, section 29.

1. Competitors must exercise sound, mature judgment, carry out all reasonable instructions from officials, obey the laws of the land and observe traffic regulations

2. Competitors must follow instructions given by the police. Failure to do so will result in disqualification and may lead to disciplinary action by the Association

3. Competitors are ultimately responsible for their own safety and for the safety of others

4. Competitors must take the responsibility for knowing the rules and abiding by them

5. It is the competitor's responsibility to be properly prepared for an event and to ensure that their equipment is suitable and fit for its intended purpose

6. It is the competitor's responsibility to know and correctly complete the full course of the event

7. Triathlon, duathlon and aquathlon are individual endurance events. Any teamwork that provides unfair advantage over other competitors is expressly forbidden

8. No competitor shall be permitted to continue racing who in the opinion of any race official is physically incapable of continuing without sustaining physical damage or loss of life

9. It is recommended that BTA members do not participate in triathlon, duathlon and aquathlon events that have not been sanctioned by the Association. BTA insurance does not cover the member while participating in such an event, which may not meet the safety standards of the Association. Participation may also render the member ineligible for selection to a national team. For the purpose of these rules this applies to Age Group, Junior, U23 and Elite teams

Race conduct

1. Competitors must conduct themselves in a proper manner and not bring the sport into disrepute

g page: A well-prepared bike rack with athlete in mid-transition.

Transition rules and regulations *continued*

14.2 All other competitors, officials, volunteers and spectators must be treated with respect courtesy

14.3 Threatening, abusive or insulting words or conduct are not permitted and competi may be disqualified for using such

14.4 All competitors must wear any official swim cap, bib or numbers provided by the organizer. These must be worn unaltered and be both visible and/or readable at all ti (See Race Numbers, section 16)

14.5 Competitors must be adequately clothed at all times, the minimum being a one or piece non-transparent swim suit together with a cycling or running top if appropriate competitors must ensure that their upper body is clothed during the cycling and run sections of the event

14.6 Race equipment must not be discarded at any point on the course but must be place the athlete's allotted position in transition

14.7 No individual support by vehicle, bicycle or on foot is permitted except as provided by organizers. Competitors may not receive any assistance other than that provided by race organizers

14.8 Parents/Guardians/Accompanying adults: Failure by a parent/guardian/accompan adult to carry out instructions from officials, or failure to conduct themselves in a pr manner may lead to disqualification of the competitor and/or disciplinary action aga the competitor by the Association. Misconduct by a parent/guardian/accompanying a may include, but is not limited to:

- threatening, abusive or insulting words or conduct
- failure to obey marshals/officials instructions
- handing water bottles or any other equipment to, or collecting them from compet
- tampering with the equipment of others
- unsporting impedance

15 **Transition areas**

15.1 In order to avoid accidents, safeguard equipment and protect personal possessions, ath must not bring helpers, friends or family members into any transition area

15.2 Pets are not permitted in the transition area

15.3 Equipment must be PLACED in its allotted position and not where it may hinder progress of other competitors. Equipment that is discarded will be regarded as a hindr and a time penalty may be issued (See Penalties, section 21)

15.4 Cycles must be placed in their correct allotted position both at the start and finish of cycle section. Cycles should be racked by either the seat pin or by the handlebars/b levers unless other arrangements are provided. Bicycles which are incorrectly racked be determined as being an impedance to other athletes (See Penalties, section 21)

Competitors must mount their cycles and start riding only when the part of both wheels which touch the ground are outside the transition area (i.e., beyond the officially designated cycle start)

When returning to transition competitors must dismount their cycle before any part of the cycle leaves the 3m dismount zone, which will be clearly marked before the end of the cycle course. They may then walk or run with their bike to its allocated position

Competitors must not interfere with another competitor's equipment in the transition area

Competitors must not use any device to mark their position in transition. Any device or marker will be removed by the referee but if this is not possible a penalty will be applied (See Penalties)

Pacing/Drafting

Competitors are not allowed to draft, i.e., take shelter behind or beside another competitor or motor vehicle during the cycling segment of races

Bicycle Draft Zone

a) For all Age Group Events (except Long Distance)
    The draft zone is a rectangle measuring five (5) metres long by two (2) metres wide. The centre of the leading 2 metre edge is measured from the back edge of the back wheel. A competitor may enter the draft zone of another competitor but must be seen to be progressing through that zone. A maximum of 15 seconds is allowed to progress though the draft zone of another competitor. If an overtaking manoeuvre is not completed within 15 seconds the overtaking cyclist must drop back

b) For all Competitors in Long Distance Competitions (Elite and Age Group)
    The draft zone is a rectangle measuring ten (10) metres long by three (3) metres wide. The centre of the leading 3 metre edge is measured from the back edge of the back wheel. A competitor may enter the draft zone of another competitor but must be seen to be progressing through that zone. A maximum of 30 seconds is allowed to progress through the draft zone of another competitor. If an overtaking manoeuvre is not completed within 30 seconds the overtaking cyclist must drop back

The draft zone of one competitor may not overlap the draft zone of another competitor

Competitors may enter the draft zone of another competitor for the purpose of overtaking as detailed above or in the following circumstances:

a) For safety reasons
b) At an aid station
c) At the exit or entrance of a transition area
d) At an acute turn
e) If race officials exclude a section of the course because of narrow lanes, construction, detours or for other safety reasons

Transition rules and regulations *continued*

19.5 When a competitor is passed by other competitors, it is his/her responsibility to move of the draft zone of the overtaking competitor. Failure to do so may result in an of caution. A competitor is passed when another competitor's front wheel is ahead of his/

19.6 Side-by-side riding, while still observing the draft zone, is only allowed on courses tha fully closed to other traffic. On open, or semi-open, courses only single-file ridir allowed

19.7 Vehicle Draft Zone: Competitors are not allowed to gain unfair advantage by draftin officials' escort vehicles, TV and radio vehicles, etc. The vehicle draft zone is a recta thirty-five (35) metres long by five (5) metres wide which surrounds every vehicle on cycle segment. The front edge of the vehicle defines the centre of the leading 5 n edge of the rectangle. The driver of the vehicle, who must be appropriately briefed b organizer, is responsible for upholding the zone

19.8 In events where there are draft-legal waves the BTA will follow the current ITU rt on drafting. This may require equipment such as aero bars to be changed (visit w triathlon.org to view current ITU rules)

20 Running conduct

20.1 No form of locomotion other than running or walking is permitted

20.2 Competitors shall at all times run so that they do not deliberately obstruct or inte with other competitors, making contact other than by accident shall be declared unspo impedance

21 Penalties

21.1 Competitors may only be penalized by readily identifiable race referees

21.2 All infringements are to be reported to the senior race referee who will have the resp bility of posting penalties

21.3 Penalties may be issued or disqualifications given at any time up to the announceme the final results, except where drug testing is involved, when results must be consid provisional until test results are known

21.4 The following penalties will be imposed for infringements

Disqualification

a) Threatening, abusive or insulting words or conduct
b) Breaking road traffic regulations
c) Dangerous conduct/riding
d) Diving (but see Swim Conduct, section 17)
e) Failing to obey marshals or the police
f) Nudity

Outside assistance
Tampering with the equipment of others
Unsporting impedance, including but not limited to incorrectly racked bikes, discarded equipment and the use of marking devices which impede others
Two (2) drafting violations noted by motorcycle referee(s) or four reports from static draft-control marshals or one (1) drafting violation and three reports from static draft-control marshals. NB: There is no requirement for a draft-control marshal to indicate that a competitor has been reported
Course irregularities (unless the competitor returns to the point at which he or she left the course, or a point on the course prior to it, and then completes the course)
Breach of conduct by parent/guardian/accompanying adult

qualification if fault not rectified after a warning

Illegal equipment (swim, cycle or run equipment)
Banned equipment including but not limited to mobile telephones and personal stereos
Illegal progress (during swim, cycle or run)
Racing topless

minute penalty

Helmet violations (unclipping helmet whilst in contact with the cycle)
Number violations (not able to be altered after a warning)
Riding in the transition area
Markers in transition that cannot be removed but do not impede the progress of others
Drafting: One (1) drafting violation noted by a motorcycle referee or three (3) reports from static draft-control marshals. NB: There is no requirement for the marshal to indicate that a report has been made

the interests of safety motorcycle referees will not provide an audible or visible warning for a ting violation.

lties will be posted by the referee at the conclusion of the event.

TE: In the case of any athlete or parent/guardian/accompanying adult whose conduct is ned to be threatening, abusive or insulting, the Association will consider disciplinary action st that athlete.

Appeals

An appeal is a request for a review of a decision made by a referee

Appeals cannot be made against 'judgment calls' by officials. Judgmental calls include, but are not limited to, drafting, dangerous riding and unsporting conduct

Appeals must be made in writing to the race referee within one hour of a penalty being notified and be accompanied by a fee of £15.00 refundable if the appeal is upheld

Transition rules and regulations *continued*

30   **Control of drug abuse**

30.1   Doping is strictly prohibited and is an offence under British Triathlon Association International Triathlon Union rules

30.2   For the purpose of these Rules, the following are regarded as doping offences:

30.2.1   the finding in an athlete's body tissue or fluids of a prohibited substance
30.2.2   the use or taking advantage of a prohibited technique
30.2.3   admitting to having used or taken advantage of a prohibited substance prohibited technique
30.2.4   refusal or failure to submit to doping control
30.2.5   assisting or inciting others to use a prohibited substance or prohibited techn
30.2.6   trafficking, distributing, or selling any prohibited substances other than in normal course of a recognized profession or trade

30.3   A prohibited substance includes a metabolite of a prohibited substance

30.4   A prohibited technique includes but is not limited to:

30.4.1   blood doping
30.4.2   use of substances and methods, which alter the integrity and validity of u samples used in Doping Control

30.5   The full list of prohibited substances and techniques is contained in the Internati Olympic Committee's current list of prohibited substances and methods. Unless other amended in writing, or unless a substance is specifically included or excluded, the Br Triathlon Association and International Triathlon Union list of prohibited substances always include the most current recommendations from the IOC

30.6   The reasons for ingestion of a banned substance need not be established in order to de mine whether or not a doping offence has been committed. The International Triatl Union shall determine procedural and administrative guidelines for the conduct of do control. These guidelines are contained within the International Triathlon Union's cur 'Doping Control Rules and Procedural Guidelines'

30.7   A departure or departures from the procedures set out in the 'Doping Control Rules Procedural Guidelines' shall not invalidate the finding that a prohibited substance present in a sample or that a prohibited technique had been used, unless this depar was such as to cast real doubt on the reliability of such a finding

30.8   All competitors in competition sanctioned by the British Triathlon Association mus required, submit to doping control

30.9   Where a doping offence is reported to the British Triathlon Association, the Associa will initiate the process of review, suspension, hearing and appeal as set out in Association's anti-doping policy

0 The finding that an athlete has used any banned substance or other doping method shall result in the athlete being disqualified from the event at which the doping infraction occurred as well as from any events taking place during the interim between the testing and the outcome of the final appeal

1 The Penalties for Doping Infractions under British Triathlon Association and International Triathlon Union rules are:

30.11.1 For anabolic steroids, amphetamine-related and other stimulants, diuretics, beta-blockers, narcotic analgesics, designer drugs and any other boosting violations not specifically included in this paragraph:

    a) First Offence: up to a maximum two-year suspension
    b) Second Offence: lifetime ban

30.11.2 For Ephedrine, phenylpropanolamine, caffeine, pseudoephedrine, strychnine and related compounds:

    a) First Offence: up to a maximum of 90 days suspension
    b) Second Offence: up to a two-year suspension

30.11.3 For refusal to submit to testing:

    a) Same penalties as for anabolic steroids, etc., above

2 All prize money or other compensation gained by an athlete in events contested by that athlete after the finding of an 'A' sample positive, but prior to the final outcome of a hearing, will be held by the Association pending final resolution of the case. If the athlete is found to have committed a doping offence, all prize moneys and/or other compensation, including titles will be redistributed to other athletes according to the amended result list. If the athlete is found not to have committed a doping offence, all prize money and other compensation will be returned to the athlete within 14 days of the finding

3 At all events sanctioned by the British Triathlon Association the event organizer is responsible for the provision of facilities for the conduct of doping control as set out in the International Triathlon Union's current 'Doping Control Rules and Procedural Guidelines'

CHAPTER 6

Conditioning

This chapter is designed to take the novice triathlete through the sometimes complex decisions of what training to do, when to do it and how to plan this into the wider training programme.

PERIODIZATION OF STRENGTH TRAINING

The goal of every athlete is to peak for his or her big race on race day. The whole training programme should be aimed at peaking for the most important competitions. Just as your swimming, cycling and running training should be arranged in this way, so should the strength training. This means lifting weights with a plan!

In Chapter 1 we included a list of principles that could be applied to preparing a conditioning programme to ensure safe and effective progress. The principles outlined below, suggested by the leading conditioning coach Tudor Bompa, are designed to take you through the correct sequencing of strength development and ultimately to optimal power and/or muscular endurance.

Develop ROM at the joints

To achieve optimal muscular strength, and therefore performance, it is essential to exercise the joint through its full range of movement (ROM). A lack of flexibility around a joint or series of joints will prevent this and so limit the athlete's potential. Additionally, lack of flexibility can also promote joint soreness and pain.

Triathletes need good flexibility in the major joint areas and the develop of this is a good starting point for any at who wants to engage in a strength tra programme.

Connective tissue strength

Connective tissues are tendons and ments. Tendons attach muscles to bone ligaments attach bones to bones. In training programme muscles adapt more quickly than tendons or ligaments temptation for any athlete is to progre training schedule in line with the mus response to activity, so that the training harder as muscle soreness reduces. The of this is that the tendons and ligam which have not recovered as quickly overused. This in turn causes inflamm and soreness, which leads to reduced training. Adhering to this law require athlete to progress through the stre training programme at a slow, contr rate, allowing proper rest periods bet gym sessions and unloading weeks fourteen to twenty-one days.

Start with the core and move out

The phrase 'you cannot fire a cannon fr canoe' is particularly apt in this inst Strong core muscles (abdominals, back, hips) are essential to the work arms and legs. If the core muscles are then they provide a poor platform fo upper and lower limbs. Any long-strength programme should attemp develop core strength before that of the and legs.

lop stabilizers before prime movers

...e same way that the trunk muscles ...de a strong platform for the arms and ...well-conditioned stabilizing muscles ...e the prime movers to function more ...ively. Stabilizing muscles contract iso-...cally to fixate or immobilize a joint so ...nother joint can work. An example of ...vould be when the shoulder is fixed, ...ing the elbow to flex and extend.

...movements, not muscle

...tic performance is all about many ...le groups working together or in ...nce. There are very few examples of ...le groups working in isolation, although ...' training programmes include exer-...where the trunk, for example, is in a ...position. One of the principles stated ...r was that of specificity. Applied in this ...xt, athletes must aim to try and use ...ises that closely mimic those found in ...port to optimize muscle development. ...e are times, however, when you may ...to ignore this particular guideline, for ...ple during injury rehabilitation or when ...cting a specific muscle imbalance ...em. At such a time it may be necessary ...empt to isolate a muscle or group of ...les in the short term.

GRAMME STRUCTURE AND ...RCISE ORDER

...you have completed all of the prepara-...work it is time to write down your ...n plan(s). Regardless of the phase of ...ng that you are in, your sessions should ...s follow a similar format.

...ing frequency

...ing frequency refers to the number of ...ng sessions undertaken in a set period ...ne. There are many variables that can ...this, some of which are only relevant ...te lifters. The remainder may have some ...when preparing your programme.

- Training on three alternating days per week (e.g. Monday, Wednesday, Friday) has been shown to be the best format for previously untrained subjects of college age (Berger, 'Strength Improvement', *Strength & Health*, 1972). This suggests that at least 48 hours' recovery is necessary between sessions
- The majority of research suggests that three workouts per muscle group per week is the minimum frequency to cause maximum gains in strength
- Athletes seem to recover more slowly from multi-joint exercises than single-joint exercises
- Within the same athlete, muscles can recover at different times. For instance the upper body muscles seem to recuperate more quickly from heavy loading sessions than lower body muscles
- As the lifter gains more experience, and is able to tolerate a greater workload, frequency can then be increased
- Resistance training once every ten to fourteen days will be sufficient to maintain strength levels for many weeks

These guidelines generally talk of optimal strength and hypertrophy gains. Any training programme intended to overload the individual regularly will promote some form of improvement, though not necessarily optimal improvement.

Most of the points made above are guidelines and should be treated as such. Use the principle of individuality when writing your programme.

Load assignment

When preparing a resistance training programme a common stumbling block is the task of assigning a load for a particular exercise. How much should a person lift for a given exercise? Is there a standard load based on age, gender, training status?

If you are a novice who has never lifted, or only recently started lifting weights, then any weight on the bar will provide an overload. A more important goal in the first few weeks is to learn the correct technique and

	Calculation of load for strength training					
% of 1-RM	100	95	90	85	80	75
RM	1-RM	2-RM	4-RM	6-RM	8-RM	10-RM

become comfortable with the whole process of weight training. In this instance your choice of load for the first few sessions should be conservative. You can then gradually raise the weight every two or three workouts. Within a few weeks you will be working to the required intensity for each set.

A safe way to decide on the weight to be used is to follow this simple exercise:

- Perform 10 repetitions with a relatively light weight. Assess how easily you have completed this
- Allow a rest of 2–4 minutes
- Add more weight and perform 10 more repetitions
- Continue, always allowing a rest of 2–4 minutes between trials, until you reach 10 repetition maximum (RM), this being the level you can reach with comfort

Using the 10-RM test is safer because novice lifters may not yet have developed the balance and co-ordination skills necessary to attempt maximal lifts.

Once the weight for a given RM is known then nominating the load to be used in future workouts is a fairly simple process when using the accompanying table. The load selected will then be based upon your goals and the required intensity of the programme, depending on your strength, power and local muscular endurance (LME).

Once you have taken six weeks or so over the initial stages of training, you should be familiar with the requirements of weight training and comfortable with the basic techniques.

TRAINING FOR STRENGTH, POWER AND MUSCULAR ENDURANCE

According to Tudor Bompa, one of the most promoters of periodization, 'the mate objective of resistance training develop power or muscular enduranc combination of these factors could be te power endurance. In order to achieve we have to apply two separate training cepts, which can be easily differentiated the following analogy.

Two athletes of the same weight are to run the same distance and could t fore be said to be equally as strong. are able to apply the same force agains ground to propel them forward. If o these athletes were to cover the distanc quicker time then that one could be sa be more powerful as a result of having formed the same work in a shorter tir however these two individuals perfo work at the same rate, but one was al keep going for twice the distance, th or she would have greater muscular e ance.

Triathlon is a sport composed of skills that are usually endurance-relatec could logically argue that the dom factor in triathlon is muscular endur but nevertheless we should not overloc contribution of power or strength ir equation.

To build power and muscular endu to their optimum levels we must first de a base level of strength, sometimes k as general strength. This can be vi as the foundation for any future str development. Neglecting or underdev ing general strength can inhibit an ath eventual performance level.

UCING THE POTENTIAL
INJURY

sport of triathlon encourages high
nes of training among its athletes. The
e of the sport attracts a certain type of
n, many of whom are high achievers
ypically set themselves very high stand-
and goals. While triathlon offers the
rtunity to train in three sports instead
e, thus providing a cross-training effect,
lso increases the potential for injury. It
uncommon for athletes to try and train
they were a 1,500m swimmer, 40km
trialler and a 10km runner, and sustain
nes that one might find in specialist
sports. The outcome, unsurprisingly,
ry from overuse.

rehensive and holistic physical preparation
rove invaluable.

DEVELOPING CORE
STRENGTH

There is a popular, yet misguided, belief that
athletes should focus their training on the
region of the body most obviously needed
to succeed in the sport. If we were to relate
this to the sport of triathlon, it would involve
the athlete developing strength in the shoulders and upper back for swimming performance, and in the quadriceps, hamstrings,
gluteal muscles and calves for cycling and
running. The trunk region may receive some
attention, but perhaps only at the end of the
programme as an afterthought.

This is completely at odds with the principle raised earlier in this chapter that you
should 'start with the core and move out'.
This philosophy is based on the fact that the
core often initiates an action or enables

Exercises for core strength

	Phase 1	Phase 2	Phase 3	Phase 4
1	Swiss Ball hip extension, shoulders on ball	SB hip extension/flexion, shoulders on ball	SB hip extension, shoulders on ball, one leg balance	SB hip extension/flexion, shoulders on ball, one leg
	30–60 secs – 10 secs on, 5 secs off	1 min – 3:3:3 tempo	1 min – 5 sec balances	1 min – 3:3:3 tempo
2	Swiss Ball hip extension, feet on ball	SB hip extension, knee flexion	SB hip extension, knee flexion, one legged	SB hip extension, knee flexion, one legged (weighted)
	30–60 secs – 10 secs on, 5 secs off	1 min – 2:2:2 tempo	1 min – 2:2:2 tempo	1 min – 1:1:1 tempo
3	Squat and shoulder flexion, dumbbells	Squat and shoulder flexion, dumbbells	Overhead barbell squat	Overhead dumbbell squat
	30–60 secs	1 min	1 min	1 min
4	Swiss Ball back extension	SB back extension and shoulder flexion	SB back extension and shoulder flexion	SB back extension and shoulder flutter, scapula adduction and circles
	30–60 secs	1 min	1 min	1 min
5	Side-lying glute leg raises	Side-lying glute leg raises with external rotation	Standing glute med external rotations (against wall)	Standing glute med external rotations (against wall)
	30–60 secs	30–60 secs	1 min	1 min

	Phase 1	Phase 2	Phase 3	Phase 4
6	One leg ¼ squat	One leg ½ squat	One leg squat on bench	One leg squat on bench, opposite arm, dumbell shoulder flexion
	30–60 secs	1 min	1 min	1 min
7	Arch walks and calf raise	Arch walks and calf raise	Arch walks and calf raise	Arch walks and calf raise
	30–60 secs	1 min	1 min	2 mins
8	Side planks, on knees	Side planks, on knees	Side planks, on feet	Side planks, on feet, straight arms
	30–60 secs	1 min each side	1 min each side	1 min each side
9	Front planks, on knees	Front planks, on knees	Front planks, opposite arm and foot	Front planks, opposite arm and foot
	30–60 secs	30–60 secs	1 min	1 min
10		Step up – medicine ball overhead	Step up – barbell overhead	Step up – barbell overhead
		1 min	1 min	1 min
11		Split squat	Forward lunge	Forward and lateral lunge combination
		30 secs each leg	30 secs each leg	30 secs each leg
12		Horse stance vertical	Horse stance horizontal	Horse stance alphabet
		1 min	1 min	1 min

movement transference from the lower to the upper body, or vice versa. Hence the most important part of the body from an athlete's point of view should be the trunk region: the abdominals, obliques, lower back and hip flexors.

Understanding the importance of the trunk musculature in athletic performance is one thing. You must also be able to condition the muscles to do their job effectively. The following programmes are designed to work on core conditioning.

Developing stability

Any muscular action involves both prime movers or agonists (those muscles directly involved in creating movement) and synergists (muscles that assist indirectly in the movement). In performing a barbell curl, for example, the agonist is the biceps muscle and the synergists are the muscles surrounding the scapula (shoulder blade). Without this assistance the upper arm muscles would be less effective at their job. Thus the synergists prevent/limit unwanted movement.

If these stabilizing muscles, which are often neglected in the conditioning process, are not strong enough to do their job properly, the prime movers have to try to do the work in addition to their real mission. Ultimately they can do neither task effectively, with the result that there is too much unwanted movement and not enough power generated. This shows how important the synergists are.

Problem areas for triathletes can include the pelvic area (leading to hip and lower back pain), the shoulder girdle (resulting in shoulder joint and neck pain) and the lower leg.

Exercises to develop stabilizing muscles often require only very light resistance as the muscle groups involved are relatively small. In many cases body weight will provide a sufficient resistance in the early stages of training. Other modes of resistance can include thera-bands and stretch cords, light dumbbells and small medicine balls.

Before embarking on exercise of this type, and to help avoid injuries, it would be advisable to consult a Chartered Ph[ysio]therapist, who can assess your conditio[n] demonstrate the safest way to perform necessary exercises.

Research has indicated that some are[a] more prone to injury than others in triat[hlon] It is possible to strengthen these 'weak s[pots]' through the use of appropriate exercises. [Pro]vided you carefully observe these safegu[ards] Because the muscle groups in question [will] be called upon during global strength [work] they should be trained last in any progra[mme] or reserved for a separate training se[ssion] altogether.

Give technique a higher priority [than] resistance. Always progress carefully fro[m] stage to the next, making sure that yo[u] perform the activity perfectly at the cu[rrent] level before moving on to the next sta[ge]

The priority here is to improve funct[ion] rather than aesthetic qualities, so the [se] should not be of too great a concern t[o the] athlete.

Performance enhancement

Strength is defined as the ability to [apply] force. Exercise to enhance your natural a[bility] should form the initial phase of any [con]ditioning programme and should be se[en as] the foundation for future strength [work] As part of the long-term programme [of a] youth triathlete, perhaps lasting se[veral] years, the conditioning programme [alone] may last for up to twenty-four month[s. At] the other extreme, an athlete reintrodu[cing] themselves to resistance training af[ter a] period of active recovery may find [that,] depending on their lifting experience, [this] phase may take between four and ten [weeks] as part of a twelve-month general [pro]gramme.

One of the easiest ways to apply [this] type of work is through circuit training. S[ome] of the exercises that can be performe[d rely] upon body weight alone, whereas o[thers] require equipment, such as dumbbells. [When] preparing a circuit workout, such a[s the] samples given here, perform each exerc[ise in] turn and move down the programme [not] across.

Sample circuit training programmes

ple circuit using only body weight	Sample circuit using body weight and dumbbells
pees	Squat and overhead press
s-ups	Crunches
nches	Bent over rows
extensions	Lunges
ges	Back extensions
n-ups	Press-ups
at thrusts	Burpees
raise	Triceps kickbacks
	Kneeling torso rotations

Factors for circuit training

d	Bodyweight or a weight that can be used comfortably for the duration of the exercise
rcise per circuits	9–12 for novices, 6–9 for experienced athletes. Novices need to target as many muscle groups as possible
uits per session	Novices 2–3, experienced lifters 3–5
between exercises	15–20 seconds (just enough time to move form station to station and to change weight selection)
between circuits	1–3 minutes. The less experience you have, the longer you need to recover
quency per week	2–4, depending upon experience. Regular lifters will recover more quickly regardless of the duration of this phase of training. A progression should be included.

mal strength

uld be argued that a sport such as tri-n, in which resistance to forward ess is minimal, does not require a high of strength. There are, however, two nents for the development of this com-nt. Development of maximal strength certain level above that required during vent will result in the athlete having a greater strength reserve for any given action. Fewer muscle fibres are recruited for the task and so the action is performed far more efficiently. Hartmann and Tunnemann have ascertained that, beyond a certain level, the development of maximal strength is of questionable benefit to performance: having the strength of a rugby league player or Olympic oarsman is unnecessary. If the muscular endurance training phase is to produce optimal results, however, there must be a sufficient foundation of maximal strength to allow this to happen. Research, therefore, appears to favour some, but not too much, effort being put into developing this component.

The beauty of maximal strength training is that, because it requires relatively heavy loads with low repetitions and medium to long rest periods, the work leads primarily to activation of the central nervous system. The end result is an increase in strength with minimal hypertrophy (weight gain), as well as increased muscle coordination and synchronization.

Power is defined as the rate of doing work. Its application during a triathlon of any distance is important. Often this is needed to overcome an increase in resistance, such as a change of gradient, or when slowing down for a turn and then regaining momentum. In many cases the power required is actually power endurance because one explosive effort will not be enough. When exiting a corner on the bike it might take between fifteen and twenty pedal strokes to get back up to the pre-cornering speed (depending, of course, on how much you have had to slow down). These strokes will generate much more force and at a much higher rate than those required to maintain racing speed, and therefore involve the fast twitch fibres much more heavily.

Muscular endurance

Muscular endurance is the ability to a force repeatedly without undue fatigue. events such as the triathlon require rep muscular contraction over a long dura the dominant strength requirement is cular endurance. To develop muscular en ance effectively requires a loading simil that encountered in the activity with a number of repetitions. Bompa suggests there are three types of muscular endur short (activities of up to 2 minutes), ium (2–10 minutes) and long duration minutes or greater). Triathlon obviously into the last of these categories. In this similar sports, athletes apply force agai standard resistance such as water, peda the ground over a very long duration. E for this activity comes predominantly the aerobic system and so any strength ing should be designed to enhance this

Bompa recommends a regime of very repetitions performed non-stop with a r goal of learning to cope with fatigue. entails sets denoted by time rather than etitions and by very short rest periods, u only long enough to change equipme lifting apparatus.

You should take great care in choo exercises that closely replicate moven found in the sport. The number of exe and the work period allowed for each sh

Sample exercises for muscular endurance	
Exercise	*Specificity*
Step-up with knee drive	Applying force to the ground during running and also knee drive
Straight leg deadlift	Hip extension in running or pedal stroke
Triceps kickback	Push part of front crawl stroke
Leg curls	Pulling up on the pedal between 180 and 270 degrees the bike section
Single leg press	Similar to act of pushing down on the pedal
Straight arm lateral pulldown	Similar to the catch phase of front crawl stroke

Typical schedule for use by a club triathlete

Exercise	Weeks 1–2	Weeks 3–4	Weeks 5–6	Weeks 7–8	Weeks 9–10
1 Lunges	Use 30% load and perform 2 minutes of work progressively for each exercise	Perform the same work for 4 minutes non-stop for each exercise	Perform the same work for 6 minutes non-stop for each exercise	Perform exercises non-stop for 12 minutes of work. Repeat for exercises 3 and 4 and exercises 5 and 6	Perform all exercises for 36 minutes non-stop
2 Straight arm lateral pulldown					
3 Triceps dips					
4 Single leg press					
5 Back extensions					
6 Crunches					
Rest between exercises	1–2 minutes	2 minutes	2 minutes	2 minutes	6 minutes

Triathlon-specific factors to promote muscular endurance	
Swim	Introduction of increased resistance, such as drag shorts, hand paddles or a pull buoy
Bike	Riding in slightly bigger gear than normal, so reducing pedall rate to 60–75rpm Riding long hills
Run	Running long hills

be chosen on the basis of your individual training status and tolerance level. Since this type of work most closely resembles the intensity level of racing it should make up the final phase in race preparation. The duration of this cycle may last between eight and twelve weeks.

While the conventional form of muscular endurance training might have some merits, it is doubtful that an athlete could perform the number of muscular contractions required to simulate a twenty-five minute swim, seventy minute ride or a forty-five minute run. An alternative proposition is to allow the athlete to develop muscular endurance by building in factors specific to the sport.

MAINTAINING YOUR PROGRAMME

One of the biggest mistakes an at can make is to call a halt to the stre and conditioning work just before or a competitive phase begins. Many ath believe, wrongly, that this type of tra will detract from their competitive perf ances. In fact the opposite is true. The no doubt that the priority of strength conditioning work is reduced during competitive phase, but that does not it should be ignored. According to Be in his book *Periodisation – Theory & Me ology of Training*, the goal of stre

Three-week training schedules incorporating competition racing and resistance training																					
	S	M	T	W	T	F	S	S	M	T	W	T	F	S	S	M	T	W	T	F	S
Events 2 weeks apart	C			L		H			M		L					C					
Events 3 weeks apart	C			L		M			M		H		H			M		L			

C: Competition, L: Low or light weight, M: Moderate weight, H: Hard or heavy weight

Facing page: Stretching as part of a cool-do routine will ensure you can move the next c

training in the competitive phase 'is maintenance of the standards achieved in the previous phases'.

It is unlikely that athletes will be racing every week. Even if they have a very busy racing programme, many of these will be 'B' or 'C' races. This should mean that they can still include the resistance work in the programme.

While muscular endurance is the dominant strength component of triathlon and should be emphasized in the strength programme, this doesn't mean that power and maximal strength should be ignored. You should aim to integrate each at least once during the two- or three-week cycle between races.

In general the ideal maintenance programme should aim to use the minimum number of exercises to train the p movers. An entire strength workout be completed within 20 to 30 minutes good planning. This would equate to to four exercises, allowing between and four sets per exercise. Care shou taken when planning in hip and leg cises during this phase. If you find tha type of training fatigues the legs even then they should be left out of the gramme. At the very least core tra and stability work should remain ir schedule.

During the racing season all stre training should stop five or seven days b the major ('A') races. The exact time s be decided by athlete and coach in con tion, based on the experience of pre competitive phases.

festyle

n be difficult to balance a normal
ng life with the demands of sport. This
er is intended to give the reader a real-
nd workable model that can be applied
rk balance, rest and nutrition.

RITION

al nutrition has received much media
ion, certainly within the last decade,
reference to fashionable new ways of
; weight in the continuing search to
e the perfect body image. This media
ion has also covered issues relating to
fects of obesity and heart disease, both
ich are associated with diets with high
ake, particularly animal fat.

trition plays a key role in the optimal
and performance of those individuals
ake part in sport, particularly multi-
ine events. It is well known that muscle
es energy to exercise. This comes from
od that we eat. If the body is not fuelled
fuelled with the right foods, training
ecome difficult and performance levels
ecline.

e human body relies on six main dietary
onents in order to maintain a physical
ental state of health and well-being.

hydrates

are an essential part of any endurance
e's diet. Carbohydrates are a source of
es from the sugars and starches (for
le root vegetables) that fuel muscles
nost importantly, the brain. Once the
hydrate has been ingested in solid form,
ligested in the stomach. The resultant

product, glucose, is stored in the muscle and
liver as glycogen as well as in the form of
blood glucose. Here carbohydrates provide
a fast source of energy for the body. Typically
the body holds sufficient glycogen stores to
fuel itself for between approximately 90 and
120 minutes of exercise, depending on the
intensity at which the exercise is performed.
Many endurance athletes, irrespective of
their event, experience the sensation known
as 'hitting the wall' or 'knocking'. This is
the point during exercise when the muscle
glycogen stores have been completely depleted, and the body is in the process of
switching to burning fat as the predominant
energy supply.

In respect of the various triathlon events,
those taking part in sprint and standard-
distance (or Olympic distance) events will
typically find that they can store enough
energy to take them comfortably round the
course. Olympic-distance athletes, however,
may struggle on the run and will require
additional carbohydrates. The half and full
Ironman events, on the other hand, have
very different characteristics. Successful completion of either of these events requires
careful pacing of additional feeding, both
timing and its quantity, since the chances of
'hitting the wall' are far greater. In order to
perform movement (muscle contraction) the
body needs glucose. Due to the energy
demands of training for three disciplines,
approximately 70 per cent of an athlete's
food intake should comprise carbohydrates.

Carbohydrate is the term given to a group
of foods specifically designed to provide the
main source of fuel for exercise. The group
can be sub-divided into simple and complex
carbohydrates. Simple carbohydrates are

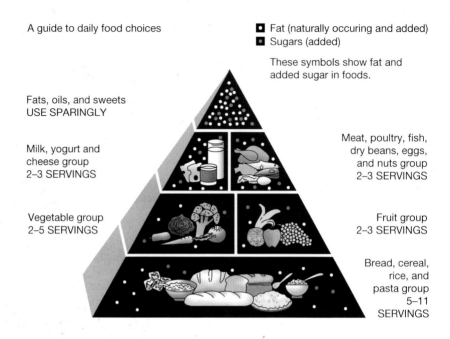

A guide to daily food choices

☐ Fat (naturally occuring and added)
■ Sugars (added)

These symbols show fat and added sugar in foods.

Fats, oils, and sweets
USE SPARINGLY

Milk, yogurt and cheese group
2–3 SERVINGS

Vegetable group
2–5 SERVINGS

Meat, poultry, fish, dry beans, eggs, and nuts group
2–3 SERVINGS

Fruit group
2–3 SERVINGS

Bread, cereal, rice, and pasta group
5–11 SERVINGS

things like table sugar, honey syrup, honey and jam, while complex carbohydrates include starchy plant foods, potatoes, rice, bananas and muscle glycogen. The difference between the two forms is that complex carbohydrates have a more complex structure at the molecular level, which affects their role in energy release.

Protein

Protein is extremely important for muscle growth, making up 20 per cent of the diet. Without it, damage to the muscle from training will not repair and strength will be compromised. Foods such as red meat (also a good source of iron), lean chicken, eggs, cheese and legumes provide an excellent source of protein in the diet. Most proteins, however, have fat as a by-product. A high-protein diet is not necessarily appropriate for triathletes owing to the slow rate at which it is converted into usable fuel in the body, since its main function is to promote energy for growth and repair to the muscles. Protein is important during the recovery phase after exercise, especially when combined with carbohydrates.

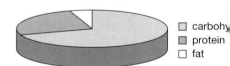

☐ carbohy
■ protein
☐ fat

Proportions of carbohydrate, protein and fa part of a healthy diet.

Fats

For many athletes this component is so forbidden. Fats, however, are good fo athlete and are essential for bodies to tion normally. Fat can only be used aerobic conditions, making it an imp fuel for endurance athletes. At res during low-intensity exercise, for exa fats are the sole contributor to e metabolism. They are the most abu source of energy in the body, with allowing you, in theory, to perform co uous exercise for up to three days. S can be found under the skin and ar

Facing page: Good nutritional preparation v guarantee you arrive at race day with the er to exit the swim shown by this enthusiastic athlete.

organs. Fat cells are also located within the muscle, to allow for the direct supply of energy for movement.

The type of fat is important in maintaining a healthy, functioning body. Animal fats (saturated fat, sometimes known as 'bad' fat) should be avoided where possible. Examples of this include fried chips, sausages, Cheddar cheese, butter, lard and fat in meat. In the long term these are the sort of foods that contribute to heart disease and high blood pressure, and should have a minimal presence in the athlete's diet.

Vegetable fats (good fats), such as mono- and polyunsaturated fats, should take up 10 per cent of your diet. These are found in, for example, avocados, olives, olive oil and nuts, such as almonds, walnuts and cashews.

Vitamins

Vitamins are metabolic catalysts that regulate specific chemical reactions that occur within the body. The essential vitamins include A, B complex, C, D, E and K. Most vitamins are chemical substances that the body does not manufacture and therefore they need to be consumed through a balanced diet. Vitamins are not a source of energy and hold no performance-enhancing function.

Minerals

Minerals are elements obtained from foods that combine to form structures in the body; a good example of this is calcium in bones. They also regulate certain body functions. Iron, for example, is incorporated in red blood cells and helps oxygen to combine with the blood cells to be transported around the body. Other examples of minerals include phosphorus, magnesium and sodium. They do not have any function in energy production.

Feeding during exercise

This is very important in order to maintain performance during exercise. Over the duration of the average coaching session, such

as an hour-long evening pool session, not necessary to consume solids in to fuel performance, since the body have sufficient energy levels. When co ering the quantity of muscle and glycogen present in the body, how consuming foods could be vital to ens that performance is maintained. These may take the form of sports gels, s bars, cereal bars, dried fruit and jam wiches. As with hydration, regular fue is the most appropriate option, altho athletes should avoid consuming large tities in one go, as this may cause ga intestinal discomfort, including bloating cramps.

Hydration

Water is one of the most important r ents in a sports diet. Two-thirds of the hu body is made up of water, which is se only to oxygen in sustaining life. Deh tion has the biggest impact on the wo capacity of muscles and temperature co of the body. During exercise, water ab heat from the muscles and helps dissip through sweat, therefore regulating temperature

Drinking too little water or losing much through profuse sweating will in athletes exercising at their maximum p tial. Because they are surrounded by w some swimmers do not see the nee drink, yet sweat rates in swimming in may be higher than in outdoor exe Failure to replace this fluid during exe can lead to heat stroke, heat coma ar serious enough, death. Unfortunately problems are quite common in endur events, such as marathon running Ironman events.

Water is a very versatile medium ir body and has many other important tions. In the blood it facilitates the t portation of glucose, oxygen and fats tc

Facing page: A bike stocked with liquid refreshment for fuelling during the cycling section.

...ing muscles and carries away the waste ...cts produced by the body, such as lactic ... In urine it eliminates metabolic waste ...cts: the darker the urine, the more con...ated the wastes. Urine is also a good ...tor of an individual's hydration status. ...r present in saliva helps in the break-... and digestion of foods.

...ver allow yourself to become thirsty. ... an athlete becomes thirsty the effects ... hydration may already have set in and ...ss of fluid may not be replaced quickly. ...y take between twenty-four and thirty-...urs to become fully rehydrated again. ...essential to have adequate fluid intake ...e, during and after exercise, or during ...petition, to prevent dehydration and a ...e in performance.

Pre-exercise hydration

Always ensure that your hydration levels are maintained throughout the day and before the training session. For an average sedentary individual (physically inactive), the recommended daily fluid requirement is about 1.5 litres of water (or eight large glasses). This may sound a lot at first, but this water may be taken either in liquid form or in foods. Owing to the physical demands placed on the body during training, however, this quantity of water would not be sufficient for a triathlete. Instead of suggesting that you count the number of glasses you consume, monitor urine output, including its colour. As a general rule of thumb, the darker the colour, the greater the level of

dehydration, which means you should drink more water. Once the colour is paler and you have become more hydrated, you should try to maintain this level of consumption. Following a training session, urine will usually be darker than normal, probably because fluid loss has exceeded input. In other words, you haven't drunk enough!

This fluid consumption may comprise a variety of liquids including:

- Water
- Cordials (e.g. orange, apple and blackcurrant, etc.)
- Fruit juices (orange, pineapple, etc.)
- Sports drinks (e.g. Lucozade Sport)
- Milk, preferably low fat
- Fruit Smoothies
- Lemonade
- Tea and coffee, preferably de-caffeinated, since the caffeinated form can actually promote fluid loss from the body, therefore dehydration.

Limit alcoholic consumption, since this can have similar effects to tea and coffee.

Exercise hydration

Sports participants often neglect this aspect of hydration. The quantity of water lost during exercise will largely depend on the environmental conditions: hot and humid environments, for example, will promote a greater loss, as will a more intense or longer coaching session. If your training sessions are around an hour in length, you should be able to complete the session quite comfortably using orange cordial, for example. This is an entirely personal decision, however, and you may feel happier consuming a sports drink. Whichever form is adopted, you should drink between 230 and 300ml of liquid every fifteen to twenty minutes. Bear in mind that this volume will increase and the rate will decrease if the session is taking part in particularly hot weather. As stated earlier, you should always drink before you get thirsty. Thirst is a common indicator that dehydration has set in, so try to keep your fluid levels topped up on a regular basis

throughout the session. Certain sports d are marketed specifically for exercise in environments, where certain essential erals or electrolytes are quickly lost, su sodium (or salt) and potassium. important that these electrolytes are n tained, as they play a vital role in m contraction.

Post-exercise hydration

To ensure that the recovery process is r mized as much as possible, post-exe drinking is vital. This recovery require replacement of the depleted energy st especially muscle and liver glycoger well as restoration of water and electr balance, as soon as possible after exer A carbohydrate-electrolyte drink can ac all these. To ensure that sufficient fluid replaced, you need to know how n you have lost. This can be determined simply by comparing your body w before and after exercise. To ensure t accurate, weigh yourself before and aft dry clothes, for example trunks or sh Post-exercise weighing in wet clothes not produce accurate results. As a ge guideline, for every 0.1kg of body w lost, 100ml of fluid should be replaced example, if your body weight drops 65.8 to 64.5kg, then you will need to re this with 1.3 litres of fluid.

Refuelling diet

No matter how hard you train, if you not refuelling your body correctly with supplies your performance will become equate. As already mentioned, the best r tional advice you can follow is alwa rehydrate with fluids and replenish glyc stores. Timothy Ackland's research sug that the sooner the athlete does this faster their recovery will be from trai and competition. Jacqui Anderson, a s dietician, writes that eating immediately exercise promotes the quickest carbohy storage. She recommends that athletes to consume 1 to 1.5 grams of carbohy per kilogram of body weight within the

Foods containing 50g of carbohydrate		
tabix	60g	(5 biscuits)
idge made with milk	350g	(1.3 cups)
ed rice	180g	(1 cup)
a or noodles, boiled	200g	(1.3 cups)
d	110g	(4 slices white, 3 thick wholegrain)
and Lebanese bread	110g	(2 pitta)
cakes	6 cakes	
nas	2 medium–large	
ges, apples and other um size fruit	3–4	
es	350g	(2 cups)
toes	350g	(1 very large or 3 medium)
	1 litre	
t' yoghurt and natural yoghurt	800g	(4 individual tubs)
oured non-fat yoghurt	350g	(2 individual tubs)
ream	250g	(10 tbsp)
	3 tbsp	
ey	3 tbsp	
a	200g	
ts drink	700ml	
ts bar	1–1½ bars	
ts gel	2 sachets	

n from J. Hawley and L. Burke, *Peak Performance: Training and Nutritional Strategies for* *t* (Allen & Unwin, 1998)

minutes of training or competition. can total between fifty and a hundred s of carbohydrate.
your glycogen becomes depleted, you ecome weak and incapable of increasing tensity or duration of training, and the f injury will increase.

RESTING

Rest is a vital part of the training process. Simply by training you are causing small amounts of damage to the structure of the body. The process of the body repairing itself is what is required for it to adapt and become stronger and faster. With rest, baseline fitness can be improved, as the accompanying diagram of the adaptation model demonstrates. The original baseline shows the starting point. As the training load is applied over time, which could be a day, a week or slightly longer, the actual ability to perform is degraded. Most people can relate to this by imagining how, in the middle of a week of tough training, you might be training hard but not in a position to perform to your best in a race.

As you rest your body repairs and adapts. It is this process that allows an improvement in baseline fitness. The diagram terms the process of rest as 'over compensation', although you may also see this referred to as 'super compensation'. The process in practice is the same: it is about training hard and recovering well, so that you can perform harder and faster next time. The diagram also shows reversibility. The principle behind reversibility is that, if you were to do no training, your baseline fitness would decline. The maintenance of fitness will be discussed in the final chapter.

If you do not rest your body will not be able to make the adaptation necessary for your baseline fitness to be improved. If this happens you will start to become overtrained. The concept of overtraining has become much more prevalent in the past few years. Awareness of its dangers has greatly improved the situation for athletes, but it has also caused a degree of confusion. The term 'overtraining' itself does not tell the whole

story. In the context of a discussion of it might perhaps be better to consider syndrome in terms of 'under-resting' r than 'overtraining'. The decline in bas fitness and the ability to perform is not essarily caused by too much training, the actual load may be relatively light. real cause of the decline in ability to per is insufficient rest.

The diagram below of the overtrai model illustrates this process. As before apply a training load from the baseline fi point, represented by the first down curve. At the end of the curve the athl fatigued and their ability to perfor degraded. Rest would here be the option, but if it is insufficient, or an tional training load is applied too soon, the baseline fitness will continue to de as is demonstrated by the second and s quent downward curves.

When illustrated like this it appears a simple process that can be easily avo That is how it should be, but it is ea fall into the trap of overtraining. A con scenario is that an athlete performs bac a race. In response to this, the very day they set about training harder tha fore. They continue to train without a until the next event, when they once perform badly. The process continues. written down this may appear con but it is commonplace among club atl active in many sports, including both athlon and its component discip

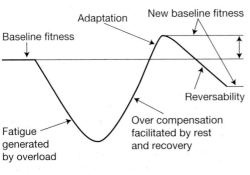

Adaptation model

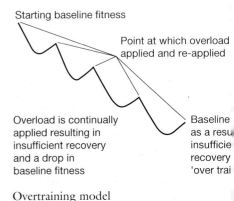

Overtraining model

...ate and well-planned training will ensure
...ny athlete of any age can compete to the
...f their potential.

...fully considered planning will ensure
...sufficient rest is included in any plan.
...st can be active as well as passive. A
...e swim, walk or steady bike ride can
...de all the rest necessary for some people.
...: individuals require only one day's rest
...ten days; others need two days' rest a
.... Finding what you need is a process
...al and error. You must listen to your
..., taking note of how you feel and
...ting your training as necessary. A little
...f ache and muscle soreness is to be
...:ted, but if this prevents you from pro-
...ing through your planned session, or
...not seem to ease after a warm-up, then
...der a bit more rest. Other symptoms of
...raining include loss of appetite and
...lity to sleep.

As a basic guideline, start with at least one very easy day in your weekly programme and one day of complete rest. Work from here and you can extend the period to ten days. You can even drop the easy day if you feel you can cope with that kind of load. If you find that from this starting point you still feel tired, you can either put in additional easy days, which are especially useful if you are trying to lose weight as well, or insert additional total rest days into the period in question, if necessary.

Other factors that will affect your ability to rest include family and work commitments. We will look more closely at working this kind of demand into your training, but be aware that if your work or family life is very demanding a rest day may not actually be very restful. Using a rest day to tackle demanding household chores, such as gardening, may not have the desired effect on your training. Remember that you need good quality rest to complement good quality training.

DEALING WITH INJURY AND ILLNESS

When considering injury prevention we need to look at the ways in which you may sustain injury:

1 Injuries relating from contact with the ground
2 Injuries resulting from contact with other participants
3 Injuries resulting from poor technique
4 Injuries resulting from unsuitable equipment
5 Injuries resulting from unsuitable clothing and footwear
6 Injuries resulting from inappropriate training programmes
7 Injuries caused by lack of fitness or sudden increase in volume
8 Injuries resulting from inappropriate training loads
9 Injuries exacerbated by lack of treatment
10 Injuries that recur owing to insufficient recovery

When an injury occurs it is often tempting to continue to train through it, ignoring the pain and hoping it will go away. It will not. If you suffer from a twist or fall then apply the RICE principle:

- Rest
- Ice
- Compression
- Elevation

If this does not have an effect on reducing pain and swelling you should seek medical advice as soon as possible by visiting your GP or a hospital. Depending on the outcome you should then seek out some form of remedial therapy. There are many sports therapists practising in the UK, although many of them have only basic qualifications

sible approach to returning to training you can still get there on race day.

of these types of injury can be pre-d by being careful and planning what re doing. Injury types 1 and 2 are gen- the result of trips and falls. While dy plans to fall, by being careful about urface you run and ride on you can e the risk considerably. Injury types 3, and 6 are all related and by following uidelines in this book you should avoid g up this kind of injury. Injury types 7 can be avoided by following the plan-and training guidelines we have estab-d and by being careful when coming from illness.

e approach to illness is similar to that turning to training after injury.

g page: By training across three disciplines, ances of injury are reduced but not ated.

When the prep goes well any athlete has the right to feel proud of what they have achieved.

and there are differing degrees of training. As with most things, local recommendations are the best, and the surest way to find a suitable practitioner may be to approach a local triathlon or single-discipline club. GPs have differing approaches to sport: some will simply tell you not to take part, others may be more sympathetic and constructive with their advice. Follow any guidelines issued by therapist or doctors and do not rush back to training, since this could cause a more serious issue and a much longer break from training. Work around the injury. If the injury is run- or bike-related, for example, then focus on swimming and core stability strength and conditioning work; if the injury is swim-related then focus o[n] other two disciplines. This is a great w[ay] keep sane and is one of the real benef[its] triathlon. Indeed this flexibility is ofte[n] reason people get involved in triathl[on] the first place.

When approaching training after an i[njury] do not be tempted to rush back in. You need to build up slowly on the recov[ery] area. You will not be able to return inst[antly] to your previous volume and intensi[ty] may need a number of weeks of ca[reful] progress to build back up to your fo[rmer] standard. Do not rush, do not take [short] cuts and do not ignore any symptoms which you may not have properly recov[ered]

ace Preparation

re now ready to prepare for your race
You could argue, however, that every-
you have done so far has been
ring you for race day. The approach we
:aken has been that, instead of training
ien looking for a race to enter, we have
he race as the overall target and focused
is one particular event. This has many
tages, but also some disadvantages. On
us side, it gives focus and a very clear
ion and time-phased goal for motiva-
purposes. On the negative side,
h, if through bad luck you happen to
on the day of the race you targeted
time ago, this might be disastrous for
overall plan and damaging to your moti-
a to carry on. This chapter is designed
ide you through the actions and activ-
with which you should be involved
g the final few weeks and days prior to
event. If your goal is a long-distance
or you have used interim events as
r goals throughout your programme,
an use some of the following sugges-
but you may not want to rest up or
your activities before each interim goal,
this may have a detrimental effect on
onger-term training programme.

ERING THE RACE

arliest form of preparation is the entry
race. If you are targeting a local race
you may already have contact details
e race organizer and be aware of the
procedures for your chosen race. If you
ravelling further afield or you are
ng a bigger high-profile race you need
ke yourself very aware of the race entry

procedures. Big race organizers, such as
London Triathlon and most Ironman events,
have their own websites that usually state the
opening date on which entries will be
accepted. Look at these sites as early as possible, since entries for many Ironman events
open almost twelve months before the race.
Especially popular events fill up very quickly
and you need to act straightaway. Details
may be found in magazines such as *220*,
while the website of British Triathlon lists
all the events run throughout the year.
Unless stated otherwise, race organizers will
be accepting entries as soon as details are
published on the British Triathlon site. The
same organization also publishes an annual
handbook early in the year listing all the
events taking place during the coming year.
Standard entry forms are available in the
handbook or may be downloaded from the
British Triathlon website. Some race organizers use their own entry forms; these can be
obtained by applying directly to the organizer. Once your race entry has been posted
and accepted you can settle down to working
on your preparation.

If you have targeted an event some distance from your home, or even abroad, you
will need to consider the travel and accommodation that you will require. This is best
tackled no later than six weeks before the
event, especially if you are targeting a large
or foreign race. When considering travel, be
aware that, whatever form of transport you
use, a long journey will leave you feeling
fatigued. If you are travelling abroad, reach
your destination at least one day before the
race, allowing yourself time to recuperate,
rest and get organized so that you are in the
best possible condition on race day. There

are a number of strategies to help you deal with problems you might encounter if you are travelling across large distances involving time differences. You could travel well in advance of the event and use a minimum of three days to acclimatize yourself to the local time zone and, if necessary, the climate. An alternative is to arrive with only one day spare, as suggested above, and keep your body clock on your own time zone as far as possible, despite the local time difference. This second option is less easy but can incur fewer costs if expenditure is an issue.

Many larger British events have a registration period on the day preceding the event. For these you will need to plan to arrive the day before. If this is the case, arrive as early as possible on that day and use the time to rest, relax and carry out some of your other preparations.

DO YOUR HOMEWORK

When looking for accommodation, first ask the race organizer for his recommendations. Many larger organizers have relationships with local hotels that provide good value for money and an environment conducive to good performance. Larger races, for example, may make hotels aware that there will be a number of triathletes staying with them and organize special rooms for bike and equipment storage. They may also organize a special breakfast so that athletes can eat as early as possible, an important consideration given the hours when races are often held.

Find the exact location of the race and select accommodation that is as close to it as possible. Any descriptions of the accommodation you find might need decoding: 'lively location', for example, may actually mean 'noisy' and a disturbed night's sleep can have a significant detrimental effect on performance the following day. Planning your travel and accommodation well in advance will make you feel organized and help remove any additional potential stress.

Some weeks before the race you will usually receive an information pack from the

race organizer with details of the race r[...]
If it can be arranged, it may well be [...]
checking out the routes for the cycle an[...]
run sections so that you are familiar [...]
the terrain and any potential tec[...]
requirements. You may, for example, c[...]
a wider selection of gears and fit tri-ba[...]
a cycle course that is very hilly or [...]
running shoes with more support and g[...]
grip for an off-road run. It is not a [...]
lem if you are only really able to chec[...]
bike and run courses on the day itself[...]
viding you are sufficiently prepared w[...]
selection of kit options so that you can [...]
with any changes to your plans that the[...]
throw up.

Tapering is a phrase that is regularly [...]
in sporting circles. This refers to the r[...]
tion in training load prior to an event. [...]
are numerous strategies that have been [...]
historically but the principle remain[...]
same to ensure that you arrive at race [...]
peak condition. This process can start [...]
as much as three or four weeks out from [...]
day. At this point it involves a reducti[...]
volume rather than intensity, meaning [...]
work just as hard but you do not d[...]
duration that you had previously been c[...]
If you are targeting a standard midd[...]
long-distance race this would mean tha[...]
plan for the increases in distance to be [...]
pleted by four weeks (*see* Chapter 1)[...]
the initial part of the taper you con[...]
with the intensity of the workouts an[...]
reduce the volume. You should probab[...]
stick to your planned frequency as [...]
During the final ten to fourteen days [...]
the race you should look to reducing [...]
training load further, probably by red[...]
the frequency of your training. Ses[...]
that have already been reduced in vc[...]
and duration should now be cut en[...]
although those that you do complete s[...]
remain as intense as ever.

This stage probably runs into the la[...]
days, during which you probably und[...]

Facing page: The final preparations will give[...]
the confidence to race.

little training at all. Any sessions you still perform should be very gentle and not too long. This is to ensure that you arrive at the event well rested but not feeling too sluggish. A gentle swim, cycle or jog will help keep the body moving and will prevent you from feeling lethargic. Do not be tempted to push hard during these sessions, even though your body will probably be asking you to and, it is to be hoped, you feel as though you can. Giving in to this could be detrimental to your pereformance on the day.

During this final three-week period you also need to pay some attention to your race kit. Many good athletes have had a less than perfect race day through checking their equipment only the night before an event, rather than weeks before. Check your running footwear to ensure that the shoes you plan to use (and also your backup shoes, if you have them) are in good order. If you do so at this early stage there will be plenty of time for delivery if you need to order replacements. Get your racing bike serviced and check your cycling shoes. It is very important that your bike is as efficient as possible. A good cycle mechanic will spot potential problems before they really manifest themselves with a failure. The plates that attach cycling shoes to the pedals can wear out, so ensuring that these are in perfect condition for race day will give you the best possible chance. Check your clothing. What do you plan to wear to race in for the swim? Will you be using a tri-suit or a two-piece outfit? Will you be racing in a wet suit, and are you familiar with how it will feel and how to get it on and off? Do you have a number belt on which to pin your numbers and, if so, does the race organizer permit their use? Is your cycle helmet in good order? Eyewear is also a consideration: are your goggles for swimming in good repair and do they fit well? Sunglasses can improve both comfort and visibility during the cycling and running stages; they also promote safety as they are good for keeping dust and flying objects out of the eyes. Do not be tempted to try out new equipment of any kind on race day. If you are planning

on making any changes, you must first proven your equipment in training. as many spare items as possible, especi you are travelling some distance. Iten get lost and a spare and comfortable s extra kit will ensure you can still race a intended.

THE LAST FEW DAYS

From about five to seven days out you to consider your nutrition and hydratio the event. This is not the time to be ning any large celebrations and it m worth carefully considering and plan what and where you will be eating ove final few days. What the body needs than anything else during this perio good quality carbohydrates and a steady of liquids to ensure hydration. This is cially important if you are travelling warmer part of the world or you are peting during an especially warm pe During your training follow the advi pre-race fuelling (see Chapter 7) and sure you are comfortable with how this and the effect that it can have.

Your lifestyle during the final week b an event can have a big effect on perf ance. If you have a manual job or shifts, look carefully at your work pla this week and consider taking some tim Undertaking some easier work, if pos may also be beneficial. Try to involv family and make them aware of what yc doing and why. This should help understand that this is not the time and play football in the park for two h followed by a couple of pints. As you been working toward this goal for time, you need to approach it with the possible chance of success.

Before leaving home to travel to the – preferably the night before – check al equipment and paperwork for the

Facing page: You are now in the final run-u the race. Do not allow a minor slip to hamp your performance.

and then check it again. Work through each discipline, making sure that everything you need is packed, including some clothing to wear directly after finishing, and that you have as many spare items as possible. Check that you have the joining instructions provided by the race organizer. If you need to pack up your bike for travel, whether by air, rail or car, use as much padding as possible. Airlines, in particular, may have their own policies on travelling with bikes. These may range from letting the tyres down and wheeling it onboard, to breaking it down and packing it in a rigid container. A good bike shop should be able to advise on this and help you understand how to put it back together. If you are faced by this kind of complication it should be resolved some weeks before, at the stage when you first plan your transport arrangements.

AT THE VENUE

When you arrive at the race venue, p ably the day before the race, you ne unpack your equipment and check everything, especially the bike, is in condition after the journey. If you reassembled your bike in any way, you s ride it for a short while to ensure tha mechanically sound and safe. You shoul now acquaint yourself with the bike c if you have not yet had the opportunity then need to register with the race c izer. Once this is completed you will b to put your bike into transition and s your small transition area. You will ger have only restricted access to your bike it is in transition, so make sure you pumped up the tyres as appropriate and any necessary mechanical preparations.

The joy of competing is enhanced by a great venue.

go into transition try to make visual
ers of the area allocated for your bike
g position. Set up your equipment in
same compact manner that you have
ted in practice. Finally pace the number
eps needed to take you into transition
the entrance you will use after the swim.
will give you the best possible chance
ding your bike after you leave the water.
nce you have set up your transition area
have completed all the registration pro-
res you can relax a little. There will prob-
be a pre-race briefing, which may be on
lay or morning before the race. Make
self aware of its location and timing.
make yourself aware of the location of
s at and around the venue, since there
en a rush for these before the race. Do
e tempted to hang around the race area
chat with other athletes for too long.

You really need to spend as much time as
possible resting on the day before the race,
so find somewhere to sit or lie and relax
before getting a good night's sleep.

In the morning rise as early as possible
and complete your ablutions before an early
breakfast. Many athletes then return to bed
for further rest before getting ready to leave
for the race. Check and double check that
you are taking everything you need. Arrive
at the race venue in good time and check
your transition area once again before famil-
iarizing yourself with the position of the race
marshals, who would not have been in place
on the previous day. Make sure you are fully
aware of your start time and position, then
head out to the start area in plenty of time

All that is left for you now is to enjoy the
race.

CHAPTER 9

What Next?

If you have just completed your race you may be feeling a little lost. Your motivation for training may be sliding and you are not sure what to do next. Regardless of whether you have completed a sprint event with a target of completion or an Ironman event with a specific target for completing in a given time, you will know if you have achieved your target. If you did, then great and well done, but if you didn't you need to look closely at why you did not. If your target was completion, was it illness, injury or an outside factor that stopped you? Is there anything you could have done to prevent it? What will you do differently next time to ensure you do finish?

Now is exactly the right time to pick the next event for you to complete. Do not be tempted to make it too soon, however, as you need at least a few weeks to recover and then a few more weeks to get back into preparation. If you want to have another attempt in the same racing season this may be perfectly possible depending on the race distance. A sprint event will require less recovery and less preparation than an Ironman event, with standard and middle-distance in between. It would not be possible or advisable to attempt another Ironman or middle-distance race in the same season, but a spring or standard-distance race may be possible, provided there is a sufficient break between the two.

If your target was to achieve a specific time and you missed this, consider by how much you were behind. The race organizer will often provide time splits for the swim, bike and run, and many races are now also able to tell you how long you spent in transitions. This can be very useful, as it allows

you to see where your weaknesses wer[e] this point you will probably also need to [con]sider if your targets were really achiev[ed] particularly on the course you raced up[on] target time based on a flat run and [a] course will be drastically increased b[y] course having hills and undulations.

This may be a factor, so compar[e] winning times with those on flatter co[urse] to give you an idea of the extra time th[at] takes in these conditions. When revie[wing] your performance always look for the [posi]tives and build on these while devel[oping] your weaknesses. Once you have iden[tified] the areas that need work, revisit Chap[ter] and start to plan for another event.

You may, however, have had a grea[t race] and achieved or exceeded your expecta[tions]. If this is the case, what now? Do you [want] to race fast, longer? If you are moving [up in] distance for anywhere between sprin[t and] long-distance events, use the formu[la of] adding 10 per cent per week (*see* Chap[ter]) to give a really good basis for the plan[ning] required once you have identified an e[vent]. This method can be used over any dis[tance] and is a good, safe way of increasing tra[ining] and developing your performance. I[f you] want to go faster, using the interval m[ethods] described in the discipline-specific cha[pters] will get you moving in the right direc[tion]. The split times from the race will he[lp] indicate where there is room for imp[rove]ment. An analytical approach to every a[rea] of your performance in the race will als[o]

Facing page: Deciding where to focus your attention next will help you maintain your enthusiasm for a great sport.

you target areas of improvement in terms of fitness or technique. A close examination of everything, including swim starts, pack swimming, turning, transition running from swim, transition to bike, bike technique and handling, and considering the psychological effect of racing, will give you a clear indication of where you need to focus your attention for improvement.

If you have not already done so, this would be a great time to get involved with a club. There are more than 350 triathlon clubs in the UK, as well as many more discipline-specific clubs, so you are sure to find a club of some description nearby that will be able to help you in some way. This will add an additional aspect to your training and help keep you motivated at a time when you may need some extra lift.

If you simply want to maintain the fitness you have worked so hard to achieve, you need to plan yourself a maintenance programme. This is much easier than planning a time-phased training programme with the target event in mind, since it is simply a case

of using the time planner we used in planning section and outlining a more r ageable, long-term set of training slo any given week or period.

Once you have done this you can where your sessions will be and then allo disciplines to the sessions. The good ne that, once you have achieved a level of fi and worked really hard to get there, yo not need to work anything like as har maintain the fitness level. You can drasti reduce the volume and duration of training, as well as the frequency, bu maintaining the intensity across fewer ses you will keep your fitness level. If you a long-distance triathlete you may find endurance suffers with fewer long-dist sessions but this will come back quite qu should you want to return to racing.

You are now an athlete – an experie triathlete – so keep progressing along road. Triathlon is a unique sport that al you to become a European or world cl pion at any age and over a variety of tances, so the sky really is the limit.

lossary

bic fitness
ability of an individual to undertake
ty while utilizing oxygen as a fuel.

group
way in which the majority of non-elite
es compete. Competitors are divided
ive-year age bands, from twenty up to
aged more than eighty. This allows all
es to compete to be champions within
own age groups and also to represent
country at European and world cham-
hips.

robic
ability of an individual to undertake
intensive activity beyond which the
can sustain utilizing oxygen as a fuel.

thlon
vent that comprises a swim followed
ly by a run.

ral breathing
bility of a swimmer to breathe to both
ght and the left.

m bracket
section at the bottom of the bicycle
the chainring and cranks are joined
gh the frame. This is a point that
es great stiffness.

nce
peed at which you complete a given
. The term is used most commonly in
g in referring to the number of times

the pedals revolve in any minute (revolutions
per minute or rpm). It is also used in running
to refer to the number of times the foot hits
the floor in any minute and in swimming for
the number of strokes performed in a minute.

Chainring
The large sprocket attatched to the pedals in
the centre of the bike. There are generally
two or possibly three chainrings attached to
the pedals by cranks.

Clipless pedals
Pedals that attach to the bottom of the shoes,
generally using a mechanism of springs.

Conditioning
The physical state of readiness for any given
individual.

Drafting
The practice of gaining an advantage by
racing behind somebody else. It is most effective in cycling and within 5m of the rider in
front, although there is also a benefit in the
swim and run. There are rules preventing
this in the majority of triathlons.

Drills
The practice of repeatedly performing a small
section of a skill, often in an exaggerated
form, to enhance the athlete's ability to
perform the skill under race conditions.

Dry Tri
An event of three events based within a
gym. This is usually a distance on a rowing

---

page: Racing in triathlon can become a way of life.

machine, followed by set distances on a static bike and then on a treadmill.

Duathlon
An event comprising a run, followed directly by a bike ride, and then by a final run.

Elite (athlete)
An athlete who is considered to be among the best in the country. There is no official measure of elite, but the title is generally accepted by peers.

Endurance
The ability to sustain a given workload for a long period.

Fitness
A very wide term used to describe an athlete's state of readiness. *See also* Conditioning.

Flexibility
The ability of an athlete to move a limb around the joint to its full range of movement.

Gears
The collection of sprockets used on bicycles to vary the resistnace and speed of progress. There will be a gear mechanism at the back and probably also at the front near the chainring.

Headset
The section where handlebars and stem meet the frame of the bike and swivel. It contains bearings at the top and bottom to facilitate the steering.

Hydration
The liquids that you drink and the state of hydration they provide. A well-hydrated individual would have consumed sufficient appropriate liquids to sustain life and activity at an optimal level.

Intensity
The level at which you undertake a given action or exercise. Working very hard at an activity would be an intensive workout, whereas swimming, cycling or running very easily would constitute a low intensity.

Interval training
The practice of using small intervals of within a training session during w training is very hard. This is to replicat demands of racing in small chunks, th fore helping the athlete improve.

Ironman
This refers to a long-distance race 3.86km (2.4 miles) ocean swim, 180km miles) bike race and 42.16km (26.2 n run. Ironman is a registered tradename

Lactate threshold
The highest intensity at which the body function before the production of lactic exceeds the ability of the body to repr lactic acid.

Lactate tolerance
As an athlete becomes fitter they can op at a greater intensity before they reacl lactate threshold.

Lactic acid
The waste product produced within muscles when the body operates anaer ally.

Mass start
An event in which a large number of p start at once rather than at set intervals, as every minute. This may be all compe starting at once or they may be divided groups often referred to as waves.

National governing body
The body that represents the interests particular sport in that country. W Britain triathlon is governed by the B Triathlon Association (BTA). Above th the European and international triat unions. To compete at national cham ship level or above you must be a me of your national governing body.

Non-drafting
An event at which drafting is not allow

Nutrition
The food that you eat.

水 water
ce of water, such as a lake, reservoir,
r river, that is used for swimming. An
)or pool would not be considered to
)en water.

)dization
practice of planning a training pro-
me over a long period, such as a year,
issigning titles and objectives to dif-
t periods.

belt
It worn with the sole purpose of dis-
ig a race number so that it can be moved
the back during the cycle section to
ont during the run.

le height
ured from the top of the pedal axles to
)p of the saddle. This is not to be con-
with frame height.

it
-out effort at top speed.

it distance
ce that is much shorter in distance.
ly speaking it is a race of half distance
standard distance but often the dis-
s are much shorter.

lard distance
race distance competed over in the
pic Games. Often referred to as Olym-

pic distance. The race comprises a 1,500m
swim, 40km bike and 10km run.

Static trainer
A device, normally an A frame, that holds
the back wheel of a bicycle while applying a
roller to the wheel for resistance. Often
referred to as a turbo trainer.

Strength
Term used as a shorter form of maximal
strength (the ability of an individual to complete a given workload in very short amounts)
or muscular strength and endurance (the
ability of an individual to sustain a workload
for an extended period).

Transition
The area in triathlon where your equipment
will be stored and that you will enter and
exit between disciplines.

Trisuit
A specially made suit in one or two pieces
that is used for the entire duration of a triathlon, so speeding up the transition process.
During the swim it may be worn underneath
a wetsuit if the conditions require one.

Wetsuit
A suit made from neoprene used for swimming. It is designed to trap a layer of water
between the body and the suit, which is then
warmed by the body.

Useful Addresses and Websites

International Triathlon Union (ITU)
#221, 998 Harbourside Drive
North Vancouver, BC
Canada
V7P 3T2
www.triathlon.org

European Triathlon Union (ETU)
H-1143
Budapest
Istvanmezei ut 1-3
www2.triathlon.org/etu-website

British Triathlon
PO BOX 25
Loughborough
LE11 3WX
Tel: 01509 226 161
Fax: 01509 226 166
www.britishtriathlon.org

Triathlon Scotland
Jacqueline Dunlop
Glenearn Secretarial
Glenearn Cottage
Edinburgh Road
Port Seton
EH32 0HQ
Tel & fax: 01875 811 344
www.tri-scotland.org

Welsh Triathlon
Flat 1 Stonehouse
Heol-y-Cawl
Dinas Powys
Vale of Glamorgan
Wales
CF64 4AH
Tel: 07870 612 344
www.welshtriathlon.com

World Triathlon Corporation (Ironman)
43309 US Highway 19
North Tarpon Springs
FL 34689
Tel: (727) 942-4767
Fax: (727) 942-1987
www.ironmanlive.com

British Cycling
National Cycling Centre
Stuart Street
Manchester
M11 4DQ
Tel: 08708 712 000
Fax: 08708 712 001
www.britishcycling.org.uk

UK Athletics
Athletics House
Central Boulevard
Blythe Valley Park
Solihull
West Midlands
B90 8AJ
Tel: 0870 998 6800
Fax: 0870 998 6752
www.ukathletics.net

ASA
Harold Fern House
Derby Square
Loughborough
Leicestershire
LE11 5AL
Tel: 01509 618 700
Fax: 01509 618 701
www.britishswimming.org

dex